ASCHENDORFFS VOKABULARIEN ZU
FREMDSPRACHIGEN TASCHENBÜCHERN

HERAUSGEBER HANS WINDMANN

NEW AMERICAN DRAMA

Edward Albee
THE AMERICAN DREAM

Jack Richardson
GALLOWS HUMOUR

Murray Schisgal
THE TYPISTS

Arthur Miller
INCIDENT AT VICHY

Erläutert von
Heinz Ludwig

ASCHENDORFF - MÜNSTER

Diesen Erläuterungen
und allen Seitenangaben liegt die folgende ungekürzte
englische Taschenbuchausgabe zugrunde:

PENGUIN PLAYS
NEW AMERICAN DRAMA

Penguin Books No 048066

Penguin Books Ltd, Harmondsworth, Middlesex, England, 1966

2./3., verbesserte Auflage

© Aschendorff, Münster Westfalen, 1978 · Printed in Germany

Alle Rechte vorbehalten, insbesondere die des Nachdrucks, der fotomechanischen
oder tontechnischen Wiedergabe und der Übersetzung. Ohne schriftliche
Zustimmung des Verlages ist es auch nicht gestattet, aus diesem urheberrechtlich
geschützten Werk einzelne Textabschnitte, Zeichnungen oder Bilder mittels
aller Verfahren wie Speicherung und Übertragung auf Papier, Transparente,
Filme, Bänder, Platten und andere Medien zu verbreiten und zu vervielfältigen
Ausgenommen sind die in den §§ 53 und 54 URG genannten Sonderfälle.

Aschendorffsche Buchdruckerei, Münster Westfalen, 1982

ISBN 3-402-02833-6

TABLE OF CONTENTS

Preface V

Edward Albee's Life and Work 1

Jack Richardson and Murray Schisgal 3

Arthur Miller's Life and Work 8

Select Bibliography 11

Abbreviations used in the Vocabulary 15

VOCABULARY OF THE INTRODUCTION 16

VOCABULARY OF "THE AMERICAN DREAM" 37

VOCABULARY OF "GALLOWS HUMOUR" 61

VOCABULARY OF "THE TYPISTS" . . . 108

VOCABULARY OF "INCIDENT AT VICHY" 119

PREFACE

This series of booklets is meant to help pupils and students of English to enjoy reading contemporary English and American authors in unabridged and original pocketbook editions.

As the student is spared the unprofitable and tedious work of looking up long lists of words in the dictionary, he can focus his attention exclusively on what the author has to say. Moreover the vocabulary of this booklet will offer him an opportunity to enlarge his word-power by trying to retain as many expressions as possible as he goes along with the reading. In general, he will find all those words explained that are not contained in the four basic frequency groups, as compiled by Alfred Haase[1].

On various occasions, however, it was necessary to include words of lower frequency groups, if they occur in a context which might offer difficulties to youthful readers.

A short introduction to the lives and works of Albee and Miller and a select bibliography are included; they are meant to help those students who would like to make some further studies on their own. There are, unfortunately, no studies available, so far, on Richardson and Schisgal so that the students will break new ground when reading their plays.

[1] Alfred Haase, Englisches Arbeitswörterbuch. Der aktive englische Wortschatz in Wertigkeitsstufen und Sachgruppen. Frankfurt am Main, ²1961.

Edward Albee

Edward Franklin Albee was born in Washington, D. C., on 12th March 1928. When he was two weeks old, he was adopted by Reed and Francis Albee. His foster father was the owner of a chain of theatres, and he was immensely rich. According to the account of an American magazine Albee's childhood was a time of "servants, tutors, riding lessons; winters in Miami, summers sailing on the Sound; there was a Rolls to bring him to matinées in the city; an inexhaustible wardrobe housed in a closet big as a room."[1]

In spite of all this wealth, it seems that the family life of Albee's parents was far from happy. It is generally accepted that his father was completely dominated by his wife, who was twenty-three years younger and a full foot taller than her husband. She was an avid athlete and is remembered "striding around in riding clothes". Grandma Cotta, Mrs Albee's mother, seems to have been the only person with whom Albee was very close. Elements of these early childhood remembrances will be reflected by Mommy, Daddy, and Grandma in Albee's play "The American Dream".

Albee's education was rather erratic. That is partly due to the fact that the Albees spent many of their winters in Florida so that the boy was transferred from school to school. Edward's academic performance was consequently extremely poor, and he is said to have been

---

[1] "Who isn't Afraid of Edward Albee?", Show, February 1963, p. 83.

1 Ludwig, New American Drama

dismissed from no less than three private schools within five years. The last of these schools was Choate School, at Wallingford, Connecticut, where Albee spent the only happy years of his school life. During the two years of his stay, he contributed quite a number of poems and his first one-act play SCHISM to the Choate Literary Magazine. After his graduation from Choate, in 1946, he spent brief periods at Trinity College, at Hartford, Connecticut, and at Columbia University.

Albee wanted to become a writer, but his parents did not agree; so, after a final row in 1950, he set up an apartment in Greenwich Village, Manhattan. There he went through quite a number of jobs, although his grandmother had established a trustfund from which Albee received a monthly income of 250 dollars. Thus he was an office boy for an advertising firm, a writer of music programs for a New York radio station, he sold records and books for two New York establishments, and he ran messages for the Western Union. During that time, Albee made the acquaintance of William Flanagan, who was later to compose the music for Albee's one-act play "The Sandbox". We know from Flanagan that Tennessee Williams and Samuel Becket were Albee's favourite authors then. Thornton Wilder, whom Albee met personally in 1953, is said to have advised him to give up poetry and concentrate on drama. Albee's writing of that period has mostly remained unknown.

In 1959 Albee achieved his first breakthrough with the "Zoo Story". Praise and success were slow to come, however, "The Sandbox" (1960) and "The American Dream" (1961) furthered Albee's reputation as a playwright. The first full-scale Broadway success came with "Who's Afraid of Virginia Woolf?" in 1962. From then on Albee's fame was firmly established, although the following plays did not so fully succeed. The reason for it may be due to the fact that Albee never stopped experimenting with new material and new techniques. Thus his audience was as often as not left puzzled with each new play. "The Ballad of the Sad Café" (1963) is the adaptation of a novel of Carson McCullers. In "Tiny Alice" (1964) Albee still deals with his favourite subject that a sensitive man is sacrificed to the will of a dominating woman. The play is not easy to understand because of its pseudoreligious symbolism and a poetic taste for mystery.

"A Delicate Balance" (1966) and "Everything in the Garden" (1967) both deal critically with modern society, the former tries to show that "friends may remain friends and families may retain their unity so long as no great demands are made on personal relationships"[1], the latter "attacks American materialism by presenting well-to-do suburbanites as postitutes"[2].

"Box-Mao-Box" (1968) is another play of pure experiment. The audience is baffled by an empty stage, deliberate repetitions, and language detached from the story.

Albee's latest play is "All Over", it was first produced in 1971.

JACK RICHARDSON AND MURRAY SCHISGAL

JACK RICHARDSON was born in New York City on February 18th, 1934. Having graduated from Columbia University with a degree in philosophy, he continued his studies for some time at the University of Munich. He

[2] A Student's Guide to 50 American Plays, ed. Abraham H. Lass and Milton Levin, New York (Washington Square Press), 1969, p. 293.

gave up his academic career, however, when his first two plays THE PRODIGAL (1960) and GALLOWS HUMOUR (1961) had been produced and well received off Broadway. "The critics agreed that the young playwright brought a keen intellect, wit, and objectivity to the theater"[1].

"THE PRODIGAL" is a play based on the Orestes theme. It may be "interpreted as the struggle between idealism and political opportunism. The hero is pictured as a cynical, uncommitted young man attracted neither by heroism nor power. However, unable to discover a philosophy to sustain him or to resist tradition and social pressure, Orestes ends up by accepting the role of avenger."[2]

"GALLOWS HUMOUR" consists of two one-act plays that complement each other. Richardson's message is that most people do not really live because they are walled in by their daily routine. Real life is passion, adventure, in short, the unexpected. We all hanker after it, but, at the same time, we are afraid of it.

In the first part, Walter, a one-time lawyer, now in a death cell, is offered the comfort of a prostitute for his last hour on earth. But unexpectedly Walter refuses to touch her. He has already mapped out his life down to the last minute, and he is afraid that passion might tear down the wall he has so carefully erected between himself and real life. When he was still a lawyer he

---

[1] THE READER'S ENCYCLOPEDIA OF AMERICAN LITERATURE by Max J. Herzberg, New York, ³1964.
[2] THE READER'S ENCYCLOPEDIA OF WORLD DRAMA, ed. by John Gassner and Edward Quinn, Methuen & Co Ltd, London 1969, p. 711.

believed in order and justice, until one day he lost a dead-sure case simply because his client began to hiccup at the wrong moment. This fact shattered his belief completely, and he began to run wild. He ended up killing his wife and was duly sentenced to death. From that moment things fell back into place again. Walter regained his old belief that life was order and justice. Lucy's arrival, however, reminds him of what life really is and he shrinks away from her. Lucy seems to have come in vain, but, as she puts it, "No one is lucky enough to fool himself that way forever".[3]

In the end, Walter gives way to passion, and thus he becomes alive once more before his death. He has enjoyed the chalice of life to the very dregs.

In the second part of the play, Philip, the executioner, is dissatisfied with the drabness of his life, but he has been afraid so far to break away from it, because he has felt responsible for his wife. Suddenly he finds out that his wife has been unfaithful to him for years, and he realizes with shock that he is free. He has at long last found "the crack in the wall that being Martha's husband has built around" him[4]. He will be able to realize his long-cherished dreams of adventure. He has always sensed that life is something beyond his experience, because whenever he put criminals to death he recognized that there was "a light in their eyes, a pulse behind their ears"[5] that beat faster than his. So Philip will leave his wife and his middle-class respectability that has prevented him from living. Try as he might, however,

---

[3] Gallows Humour, Part I, p. 94.
[4] Gallows Humour, Part II, p. 107.
[5] Op. cit. p. 110.

he cannot open the (symbolic) door that leads to freedom, nor can he (symbolically) kill his wife whom he recognizes as the one great obstacle on his way out. He does not realize that he is, subconsciously, afraid of the unknowm life. His wife, full of triumph, makes him see his plight: "You're the one that is keeping it (= the door) shut. If you really wanted to leave, it would spring open like a hungry mouth."[6] Through his wife's cunning Philip is kept in the old rut of everyday life. Philip's desperate question "But isn't there any chance for me at all?" is answered evasively in Martha's matter-of-fact way: "Keep bundled up, dear. Don't work too hard. And tonight- tonight we'll have something very special for dinner. Something you really like, dear, something you really, really like."[7] Philip will go on living, but he will be far from being alive.

"SCHISGAL, MURRAY[8] (born 1926). American playwright. Born in New York City, Schisgal graduated from Brooklyn Law School (LL.B 1953). During his two years of working in a law office in Manhattan and three years of teaching English at JAMES FENIMORE COOPER JUNIOR HIGH SCHOOL in Eeast Harlem, Schisgal wrote novels and plays. In 1960 The British Drama League produced three one-act plays — THE TYPISTS, THE POSTMAN (retitled THE TIGER), and A SIMPLE KIND OF LOVE STORY; a longer play, DUCKS AND LOVERS was produced in London in 1961. The double bill of THE

---

[6] Op. cit. p. 117.
[7] Op. cit. p. 120.
[8] Quoted from A HANDBOOK OF CONTEMPORARY DRAMA by Michael Anderson and others, Pitman Publishing, London 1972, pp. 400/401.

TYPISTS and THE TIGER was very successful in New York in 1963 . . .

KNIT ONE, PURL TWO was presented in Boston in 1963. LUV, another extraordinarily successful play, opened in London in 1963 and New York in 1964. JIMMY SHINE was produced in New York in 1968 for a short run.

All of this work is comedy bordering on farce, black humor, and absurdity, but with enough pathos to appeal to large audiences . . ."

In THE TYPISTS Schisgal makes use of a time-lapse technique that has already been employed by Thornton Wilder in THE LONG CHRISTMAS DINNER. The whole span of life of the two typists Sylvia and Paul is condensed into one workday. They start out in their twenties full of hope and gross self-deceptions and they leave their office in their sixties, disillusioned and resigned. Their lives are so ordinary, so devoid of any excitement that one is puzzled, at the end, over the futility of life.

Arthur Miller

Arthur Miller was born in New York City on 17th October 1915 into a Jewish family of Austrian origin. His father was a clothing manufacturer. The family then moved to Brooklyn where Miller graduated from Lincoln High School in 1932. His highschool career was unimpressive. He was much better at football than at his academic studies. The Great Depression having limited the family resources, Miller had to work in a warehouse for spare automobile parts, before he could enter the University of Michigan in 1933. At university he majored in journalism and English literature. He also followed classes in playwriting, and encouraged by his teacher Kenneth Rowe, Miller wrote his first play "The Grass still Grows" and won the Avery Hopwood Award. He completed his university career with a part-time job as a journalist and an allowance from the National Youth Administration.

In 1938 he returned to New York and continued to write, but could not make a living by it yet. So he held various jobs: he was a worker in a box factory, an employee in the Navy Yard, a truck-driver, a writer, a crewman on a tanker, and a writer of radio scripts.

In 1945 he published his first novel "Focus", a somewhat ironical study of racial prejudice. A man is discriminated against simply because he looks like a Jew, and in the end he identifies himself with the Jews and no longer refuses to undergo the same torments. Miller's first success came, in 1947, with "All my sons", a family tragedy as the afthermath of World War II. Still greater success, however, the Pulitzer Prize for drama, and international renown was achieved by "Death of a Salesman"

(1949), which had a long run on Broadway. The play is a good exemplification of Miller's theory that tragedy in the modern theatre ought not to deal with kings and noblemen, as in former times, but with common man. "... an ordinary modern individual can serve equally well as tragic hero, if he wants something intensely enough to give up everything else in its pursuit."[1] Willy Loman, the hero of "Death of a Salesman", ist a greying and unimpressive salesman who wants to provide well for his sons, and who even lays down his life in order to secure this aim.

In 1951 Miller adapted Ibsen's play "An Enemy of the People" for the American stage, it did not enjoy much success, however.

"The Crucible" (1953) is a remarkable play, although its technique is again conventional. The action is based upon the trials for witchraft that occurred in Massachusetts in 1960. The message of the historical play is true of all times, however, it shows that fanaticism of any kind does not only destroy freedom of thought, but human dignity in general. This play may have been Miller's indirect attack on senator McCarthy who had launched a campaign against so-called "un-American activities" and who had ruined many a career by simply suspecting citizens to be Communists. Miller himself was cited before a Congressional Committee, and when he failed to cite any names of people who were thought to have been engaged in radical activities, he was convicted for contempt of Congress.

Two short plays were produced in 1955. "A Memory of two Mondays" recalls Miller's remembrances of the

---

[1] J. Th. Nourse, Arthur Miller's The Crucible, New York, 1965, p. 6.

auto-parts warehouse, and "A View from the Bridge" deals with the conflict of family members of two generations with tragic ending. The Background of the play is Brooklyn.

The next decade was filled with personal difficulties. Apart from his difficulties with Congress, Miller had marital difficulties as well. In 1956 his first marriage broke up, and in the same year he married the famous American filmstar Marilyn Monroe. With her in mind he adapted his story "The Misfits" for a film scenario. The film came out in 1961, and one year later Miller's second marriage ended in divorce. A few weeks later, Marilyn Monroe committed suicide.

These personal experiences are strongly reflected in "After the Fall" (1964). Quentin, the hero of the play, is a lawyer who reviews his life. He is obsessed by feelings of guilt and frustration. All the action of the play takes place in the hero's head. All the characters quickly appear and disappear with his thoughts. One of the characters is Maggie, a drug-addicted singer, who can easily be identified with Marilyn Monroe. Many critics took offence at this sort of private revelations and considered them tactless. Time will show whether Miller's play will outlive these moral prejudices.

The theme of guilt and responsibility recurs in "Incident at Vichy" which appeared in the same year as "After the Fall". In this play ten prisoners are being held in a place of detention because they are suspected of being Jews. An Austrian Catholic prince is among them. He has been arrested in error.

In the course of the play he will be made to realize "that all who do not actively oppose the persecution of others are partially responsible for the resultant horrors"². The prince recognizes his guilt and risks his life for others in order to secure his personal dignity.

Miller's latest plays are "The Price" (1968) and "The Creation of the World and Other Business" (1972).

² Nourse, J. Th., Arthur Miller's The Crucible and ..., New York, 1965, p. 12.

Select Bibliography

A. EDWARD ALBEE

I WORKS

1. THE ZOO STORY AND OTHER PLAYS
   London (Cape) 1962
   Harmondsworth (Penguin 048.058 7) 1971 in ABSURD DRAMA
   Frankfurt/Main (Hirschgraben 6605) 1976 in READING MODERN DRAMA

2. THE AMERICAN DREAM
   Harmondsworth (Penguin 048.066 8) 1966 in NEW AMERICAN DRAMA

3. WHO'S AFRAID OF VIRGINIA WOOLF?
   Harmondsworth (Penguin 048.061 7) 1965

4. THE BALLAD OD THE SAD CAFÉ
   London (Cape) 1965

5. TINY ALICE, BOX AND QUOTATIONS FROM CHAIRMAN MAO TSE-TUNG
   Harmondsworth (Penguin 048.110 9) 1971

II CRITICAL STUDIES OF *Albee* AND HIS WORK

1. BIGSBY, C. W. E., ALBEE, Edinburgh (Oliver and Boyd) 1969
   A concise introduction to Albee's life and work that can be highly recommended as it is written with great understanding and deep insight. There is a comprehensive bibliography at the end of the book. An interpretation of "The American Dream" (nearly identical with the one in "Confrontation and Commitment") is on pp. 31/35.

2. BIGSBY, C. W. E., CONFRONTATION AND COMMITMENT,
   A Study of Contemporary American Drama 1959–1966
   Columbia, Missouri (University of Missouri Press) 1967. Bigsby surveys the development of American drama from Tennessee Wil-

liams to Arthur Miller. As far as Albee's drama is concerned, Bigsby points out that it differs essentially from the European Theatre of the Absurd.

A German translation of Bigsby's article is available in
FISCHER BÜCHEREI DES WISSENS, Bd. 6031,
AMERIKANISCHE LITERATUR DES 20. JAHRHUNDERTS,
Bd. 2, Lyrik und Drama, Frankfurt a. Main (Fischer Verlag) 1972, pp. 288/308

3. BRAUN, H. M., *Albee*, VELBER (Friedrichs Dramatiker Bd. 63) 1968
   A good and helpful introduction in German language. It is easily available. "The American Dream" is dealt with on pages 63/71.

4. STUGRIN, Michael, EDWARD ALBEE'S TINY ALICE AND OTHER WORKS A Critical Commentary
   NEW YORK (Monarch Press 671-00913-3) 1973
   A very helpful and handy book for teachers and students. After a short introduction to Albee's life, the author gives a critical study of Albee's main works including plot discussions, character analyses, surveys of criticism, essay questions and model answers. There is also a comprehensive bibliography at the end of the book.

5. RAZUM, Hannes, EDWARD ALBEE UND DIE METAPHYSIK in Lohner/Haas, Theater und Drama in Amerika, Erich Schmidt Verlag, Berlin 1978, pp. 353/363 (in German)
   Razum's study contributes largely to the understanding of Albee's plays by relating them to experiences of Albee's life. He then concentrates on the metaphysical question in TINY ALICE and shows that there is a religious symbolic meaning latent in the interrelation and interaction of the characters, by which Albee explores the mysterious nature of faith.

B. ARTHUR MILLER

I WORKS

1. COLLECTED PLAYS (containing: All my Sons; Death of a Salesman; The Crucible; A Memory of Two Mondays; A View from the Bridge; also a long and helpful introduction by the playwright himself) NEW YORK (The Viking Press) 1958

2. ALL MY SONS
   Harmondsworth (Penguin 048.029 3) 1960
   Frankfurt am Main (Diesterweg 4037) 1962

3. DEATH of a SALESMAN
   Harmondsworth (Penguin 048.028 5) 1962
   Frankfurt am Main (Diesterweg 4134) 1964

4. THE CRUCIBLE
   Harmondsworth (Penguin 048.078 1) 1965

5. A MEMORY OF TWO MONDAYS AND VIEW FROM THE BRIDGE
   New York (The Viking Press) 1955

6. INCIDENT AT VICHY
   Harmondsworth (Penguin 048.066 8) 1966
   New York (The Viking Press) 1965 (Paperback)

7. AFTER THE FALL
   New York (Bantam Books) 1965 (Paperback)

8. The PRICE
   New York (Bantam Books) 1968

II CRITICAL STUDIES OF MILLER AND HIS WORK

1. NOURSE, Joan Th.
   ARTHUR MILLER'S THE CRUCIBLE and A Memory of Two Mondays, A View from the Bridge, After the Fall, Incident a Vichy
   NEW YORK (Monarch Press 6 671-00687-8) 1965
   This is the most helpful book for teachers and students. It contains a concise appreciation of Miller's development as a playwright, plot analyses of the different plays quoted in the title, critical apprecia-

tions, character analyses, essay questions and model answers and a very good bibliography for further studies. An interpretation of "Incident at Vichy" is on pages 82/94.

2. LÜBBREN, R., MILLER (Friedrichs Dramatiker Bd 19)
VELBER 1969²
A very good introduction to Miller's life and work in German language. An interpretation of "Incident at Vichy" is on pages 102/113. The book is easily available. A bibliography is at the end of the book.

C. BOOKS DEALING WITH MODERN THEATRE IN GENERAL

1. Bigsby, C. W. E., CONFRONTATION AND COMMITMENT
A Study of Contemporary American Drama 1959–1966 Columbia Missouri (University of Missouri Press) 1967 (Cf. Critical Studies of Albee)

2. Lumley, Frederick
NEW TRENDS IN 20th CENTURY DRAMA
London (Barrie and Rockliff) 1967

3. Phillips, Elizabeth C.
Rogers, David
MODERN AMERICAN DRAMA
New York (Monarch Press 671-00854-4) 1966
(Richardson and Schisgal are not included)

4. Esslin, Martin
THE THEATER OF THE ABSURD
Garden City, New York (Doubleday and Company) 1969²
Esslin deals with the Theatre of the Absurd as a whole. There is no information on Miller, Richardson, Schisgal, and only little information on Albee.
A German translation of the book is available in Rowohlts deutsche Enzyklopädie, Bd 234, Das Theater des Absurden,
Reinbek bei Hamburg, 1965

Abbreviations used in the Vocabulary

Am	American English
adj	adjective
B. E.	British English
colloq	coloquial English
e. g.	exempli gratia (= for example)
esp.	especially
i. e.	id est (= that is)
med	medical expression
pl	plural number
s. b.	somebody
sg	singular
sl	slang
s. o.	someone
s. th.	something

NEW AMERICAN DRAMA

Introduction

p. 7

originated on Broadway [ɔ'ridʒi, neitid]	most modern plays were first performed on Broadway, the centre of the New York entertainment industry	nahmen am Brodway ihren Anfang
a subsidized cultural complex ['sʌbsidaizd]	a cultural centre receiving financial assistance from the state	ein subventioniertes Kulturzentrum
to design [di'zain]	to plan	planen, entwerfen
an alternative to [ɔ:l'tə:nətiv]	another possibility	eine Alternative zu ..., eine Wahlmöglichkeit
to lash s. th.	to attack violently by blows or words	geißeln, scharf tadeln
Time Square	a square in New York City formed by the intersection of Broadway and 7th Avenue; the City's entertainment district	
Time Square set	a group of critics favourable to whatever was produced on Broadway	etwa: die Time Square Clique

rancorous ['ræŋkərəs]	full of a deep and long-lasting feeling of bitterness	erbittert, boshaft, giftig
glamourous ['glæmərəs]	full of charm and enchantment	bezaubernd (schön)
to mourn s. th.	to feel grief for s. th.	etwas betrauern
diatribe ['daiə,traib]	bitter and violent attack in words	Schmährede, -schrift
to muster (up) sympathy	to have friendly feelings for	Sympathie aufbringen
bubonic plague [bju:'bɔnik 'pleig]	a contagious malignant epidemic disease	Beulenpest
decline [di'klain]	continued loss of strength	Zerfall, Abstieg
to coincide (with) [,kəuin'said]	to happen at the same time	zusammentreffen mit, zusammenfallen mit
a civic theatre	a theatre financed and run by a city	städtisches Theater
boom	sudden increase in activities	Aufschwung
Ford and Rockefeller foundations	here: funds of money destined to support theatre companies	Ford- und Rockefellerstiftungen
to create an impasse ['æmpɑ:s]	to bring about a situation from where there is no way out	eine ausweglose Situation schaffen
grasping [ɑ:]	greedy for money	geldgierig
trade union	organized association formed to protect the interests of its members	Gewerkschaft
rot	here: decay	Zerfall, Auflösung

aesthetics [iːsˈθetiks]	branch of philosophy that tries to make clear the laws and principles of beauty	Aesthetik, Lehre vom Schönen
to intertwine [ˌintəˈtwain]	to twist together	(sich) verflechten, miteinander verschlingen
remotely connected with	having only slight connections with	entfernt verbunden sein mit
dim	lacking keenness of intelligence	schwer von Begriff, langweilig
pot-bellied	having a thick belly	dickbäuchig

p. 8

realtor [ˈriːəltə]	B. E. real estate agent	Grundstücksmakler
to hanker for/after	to have a strong desire for	sich sehnen, verlangen nach
a sure fire hit	a play that is certain to catch on	ein todsicherer Knüller
a trend-setter	one who sets the trend in a fashion	Tonangeber, Schrittmacher
block booking	a whole set of tickets handled as a unit	Kartenverkauf en bloc, geschlossener Verkauf
fare [fɛə]	food provided for the table; here: the quality of the plays	Kost; hier: Art der Stücke
adjunct [ˈædʒʌŋkt]	s. th. extra, but subordinate	Beigabe, Zusatz
to cater for/to [ˈkeitə]	to supply amusement etc. for	etwas bieten, befriedigen

a corporation expense account	record of expenses supplied by or refunded by a business corporation	Spesenkonto eines Unternehmens
a show has become an extended gin-and-tonic	the show has become one more item one treats business friends to	die Show ist zur Erweiterung des Begrüßungstrunks geworden
gin-and-tonic	gin with tonic water	"gespritzter" Gin
genre [ʒã:ŋr]	category art or literature	Genre; literarische Gattung
offering	s.th. offered, esp. in the religious sense; here used ironically	Opfer, Darbringung; hier: Darbietung
to divert [dai′vǝ;t]	to amuse, to entertain	amüsieren, zerstreuen
at a premium [′pri:miǝm]	highly valued or esteemed	hochgeschätzt
to shun [ʌ]	to avoid	aus dem Weg gehen; (ver)meiden
dictum [′diktǝm]	formal expression of opinion; saying	Ausspruch, geflügeltes Wort
to soothe [su:ð]	to make (a person) quiet or calm	beruhigen, besänftigen
to proliferate [prǝ′lifǝ,reit]	to grow, to reproduce by rapid multiplication of cells	sich stark vermehren, wuchern
"legit" offerings [′ledʒit]	abbreviated for 'legitimate': slang for serious art (classical, semi-classical)	'seriöse' Darbietungen
distressing	causing sorrow and discomfort	qualvoll, kummervoll, peinlich

to attenuate [ə'tenju,eit]	to make thin or slender; to weaken, to reduce	dünn, schlank machen; schwächen, vermindern
bouncy [au]	showing vivacity, spirit, enthusiasm	schwungvoll, munter
fleet (adj.)	literary language: quick-moving	'flott', kurzweilig
clammy [æ]	moist, wet	feucht, naß
the clutches [ʌ]	power, control, firm grip	Macht, Kontrolle, fester Griff
Strasberg (né Freud)	ironic allusion to the fact that the man in question liked plays dealing with sexual problems	Strasberg, geborener (!) Freud
behaviourism [bi'heiviə, rizm]	doctrine that all human actions can be analysed into stimulus and response	Behaviorismus, Verhaltensforschung
assumption [ə'sʌmpʃən]	s. th. taken for granted but not proved	Annahme, Vermutung
to underlie	to form the basis of a theory or doctrine	zugrundeliegen
verisimilitude [,verisi 'militju:d]	s. th. that seems to be true; appearance	Wahrscheinlichkeit
postulate ['pɔstjulit]	s. th. that may be considered axiomatic	Postulat, Grundbedingung
to corroborate [kə'rɔbə, reit]	to give support and certainty to	bekräftigen, erhärten
explicit [iks'plisit]	clearly and fully expressed in words	ausdrücklich
mansion ['mænʃən]	large and stately house	herrschaftliches Wohnhaus, Villa

at the heart of experience	at the bottom of all experience	im Grunde/Kern aller Erfahrung
behaviour-pattern	the expected way in which some response happens or develops	Verhaltensmuster
pat phrases	expressions that one has ready at once and without hesitation	parate Redensarten; schlagfertige Ausdrücke
ambiguous [æm'bigjuəs]	of doubtful meaning; uncertain	zweifelhaft, unsicher
to topple into	to become unsteady and overturn	stürzen, purzeln
to prosper ['prɔspə]	to succeed; to do well	Erfolg haben, wohl ergehen
hoopla [u:]	game in which rings are thrown at small objects which are won when the rings encircle them	Ringwerfen (auf Jahrmärkten z. B.)
pace	here: speed, progress	hier: Tempo, Schwung
buncombe ['bʌŋkəm]	rare spelling for buncome or bunkum: senseless or purposeless talk	Blech, Gewäsch, Blödsinn
schmaltz [ʃmɔ:lts]	colloquial for sickly sentimentality	'Schmalz', Sentimentalität
to be in vogue ['vəug]	to be in; to be popular	in Mode sein
Beckett, Samuel	modern author and playwright, born in Dublin in 1906, his greatest success was 'En attendant Godot'.	

Ionesco, Eugène	born in Roumania in 1912, French dramatist, best known for his plays: 'La cantatrice chauve' and 'Rhinocéros'	
to blur [ə:]	to make er become unclear or confused in appearance	verdunkeln, verwischen, verschleiern
to reveal [i:]	to make visible, display	sichtbar werden lassen, enthüllen
nihilism ['naii,lizm]	total rejection of current political institutions and religious and moral beliefs	Nihilismus
absurdity [əb'sə:diti]	state of being unreasonable, ridiculous	Absurdität, Unvernunft
subversive [səb'və:siv]	aiming at overthrowing the established order	subversiv, umstürzlerisch
be in keeping with	be in agreement or harmony	in Übereinstimsein
to devour [di'vauə]	to swallow, to gulp down	verschlingen, hinunterschlucken
a parlour joke ['pɑ:lə]	a joke told in a private home	'Stubenwitz'
existentialist philosophy [,egzis'tenʃəlist]	influenced by Kirkegaard and Nietzsche, popularized in France by Sartre and Camus; claiming that it is the will rather than the reason that confronts the problems of a non-moral or absurd universe	

Genêt, Jean	born in Paris in 1910, modern French novelist and dramatist; his plays 'Haute Surveillance', 'Les Bonnes', 'Le Balcon'	
neurosis [nju'rəusis]	functional derangement caused by disorders of the nervous system	Neurose, Nervenkrankheit
staunch [stɔ:ntʃ]	trustworthy, loyal, firm	getreu, zuverlässig, standhaft
to swipe (colloq.)	to hit hard; noun: a hard blow	dreinschlagen, hauen; harter Schlag, Hieb
tangible ['tændʒibl]	that can be touched, clear and definite	greifbar, wirklich
verifiable [ˌveri'faiəbl]	the truth and accuracy of which can be tested	nachprüfbar
to nudge [ʌ]	to push or touch gently with one's elbow	(mit dem Ellbogen) anstoßen
metaphysical	derived from 'metaphysics', i. e. speculative philosophy	metaphysisch
to resent s. th.	to feel bitter, angry or indignant	übelnehmen, grollen
Hellman, Lillian	born 1905, plays: 'The Children's Hour', 'Days to Come', 'The Lark'	
Inge, William [indʒ]	American dramatist, born 1913, plays: 'Come Back, Little Sheba', 'Picnic', 'Bus stop'	

Miller, Arthur	American novelist and dramatist, born 1915, plays: 'Death of a Salesman', 'All my Sons'	
Williams, Tennessee	American dramatist, born 1911, plays: 'A Streetcar Named Desire', 'Sweet Bird of Youth', 'The Glass Menagerie'	
to squeeze at	to press from all sides in order to get s. th. out	quetschen, drücken
pimple	small, hard inflamed spot on the skin	Pustel, Hautpickel
implicit [im′plisit]	implied though not plainly expressed	unausgesprochen; (stillschweigend) einbegriffen

p. 10

relevant [′relәvәnt]	connected with what is being discussed	von Bedeutung für; sachdienlich; relevant
to talk real estate	to talk about immovable property such as land, buildings etc.	sich über Grundbesitz unterhalten
booze [u:] (colloq)	alcoholic drink; drinking bout	Alkohol; 'Sauferei'
lid Am (colloq)	restriction	Einschränkung
revelation	s. th. that is displayed or clearly shown	Enthüllung, Offenbarung
unrelieved cold war tension	the superpowers did not cease threatening and harassing each other	unverminderte Spannung des kalten Krieges

ostensible [ɔs'tensəbl]	(of reasons) put forward in an attempt to hide the real reasons	scheinbar, vorgeblich
trait [trei]	feature; distinguishing quality or characteristic	Charakterzug; Merkmal
flavour ['fleivə]	sensation of taste or smell	Geschmack; Aroma
to be in office	having been elected and doing the work of the government	an der Regierung, an der Macht sein
coke bottle	bottle of Coca-Cola	
the New Frontier ['frʌntjə, Am: frʌn'tiə]	that portion of American country that bordered on the wilderness and was only thinly populated by pioneers	Grenzland (zum Wilden Westen); 'Neuland'
rugged individualism ['rʌgid]	unpolished, unrefined individualism	ungehobelter, ungeschliffener Individualismus
sit-in	demonstration where demonstrators occupy a building and stay there until their grievances are considered	Sitzstreik, 'Sit-in'
orthodoxy ['ɔ:θədɔksi]	believing what is generally accepted and approved	Rechtgläubigkeit; Orthodoxie
to infiltrate ['in...]	here: to pass into people's minds without attracting attention	(sich) einschleichen, infiltrieren
vernacular [və'nækjulə]	language or dialect of a country or district; here: jargon	Mundart, Dialekt; Fachsprache, Jargon

tome [əu]	volume	Band (eines Werkes); 'Wälzer'
playwright ['pleirait]	a writer of plays	Bühnenautor
Norman Mailer	American novelist, born 1923, his first success was 'The Naked and the Dead'	

p. 11

to take up an aggressive stance [stæns]	to be aggressive in what one has to say	eine aggressive Haltung annehmen
to generalize	to draw a general conclusion	verallgemeinern
indictment [in'daitmənt]	written statement that accuses s. b.	Anklageschrift; Anklagebeschluß
to assume	to take upon or for oneself s. th. not genuine or sincere	sich anmaßen; erheucheln
to up-date	to bring up to date	modernisieren, auf den neuesten Stand bringen
Strindberg, Carl August	(1849–1912) Swedish dramatist and novelist	
bogus ['bəugəs]	sham, counterfeit	unecht, nachgemacht
Ibsen, Henrik	(1828–1906) Norwegian dramatist and poet; he criticized, in his plays, social conventions and attitudes	
overt(ly) ['əuvə:t(li)]	done or shown openly	offenkundig, öffentlich

invective [..'vek..]	abusive language, violent expressions	Schmähungen, Beschimpfungen
irrelevant [i're...]	having nothing to do with	ohne Bezug, belanglos
to fault s. th.	to find fault with	bekritteln, benörgeln
marginal virtues ['mɑ:dʒinəl 'və:tju:z]	virtues that were not mainly aimed at	am Rande liegende Vorzüge, beiläufige Vorzüge
thought-pattern	the way people are accustomed to think	Denkschema, Denkmuster
inanities of the language [in'æniti:z]	expressions that have become clichés and do not contain a real message	dummes Geschwätz; 'Plattitüden'
wisecracker	a person who makes smart and witty remarks	Witzbold
hypocrisy [hi'pɔkrisi]	pretending to be virtuous and good	Heuchelei
an old broad Am sl	an old unrespected woman	ein altes 'Frauenzimmer'
with pincers in her teeth sl	being disagreeably outspoken	mit einem gefährlichen Mundwerk
satire ['sætaiə]	piece of writing holding up persons or things to ridicule	Satire
to appal [ə'pɔ:l]	to fill with fear and terror	erschrecken, entsetzen
vapid ['væpid]	tasteless, uninteresting	schal, fade; öde
Jack Armstrong Wheaties- eater fella ['felə] Am	an eater of wheat-pancakes spelling proununtiation for 'fellow'	Pfannkuchenesser Bursche; 'Kerl'

dreamboat Am sl	an exceptionally attractive person	'Herzensbrecher'; ein 'Traum'
pal colloq	friend, comrade	'Kumpel', 'Spezi', Freund
to woo a woman [u:]	to try to win a woman	um eine Frau werben, einer Frau den Hof machen
fatuous ['fætjuəs, 'fætʃuəs]	showing foolish self-satisfaction	albern, einfältig
football toting	U. S.: betting on the winning teams in football by means of an electronic totalizator	Totospiel (beim Football mit Hilfe eines Totalisators)
orgiastic [,ɔ:dʒi'æstik]	frenzied; of the nature of wild merry-making	orgiastisch, ausschweifend

p. 12

Tea and Sympathy	a play by Robert Anderson (born 1917)	
Death of a Salesman	a play by Arthur Miller (born 1915)	
brawny [brɔ:ni]	muscular	muskulös
Happy Loman	the playboy son of Willy Loman, the main character in Death of a Salesman	
imagery ['imidʒri]	the use of images or figures of speech	Bilder(sprache), Symbolik
diagram ['daiəgræm]	drawing, design or plan to explain or illustrate s. th.	Diagramm, graphische Darstellung, Schaubild

dia-grammatic(ally)		graphisch, schematisch
conceit (in language) [kən'si:t]	humorous or witty thought or expression	guter oder witziger Einfall
flourish ['flʌriʃ]	decoration, ornament in writing	Schnörkel, Verzierung, Floskel
rhetoric ['retərik]	the art of using words impressively	Redekunst, Rhetorik
he does not tackle conformity as a concept		er geht die Konformität nicht als einen (bloßen) Begriff an
to nauseate ['nɔ:sieit]	to cause a feeling of sickness or disgust	Brechreiz, Ekel hervorrufen
nauseating		Übelkeit erregend, widerlich
repression	forcing out of the mind into the subconscious of impulses and desires, often resulting in abnormal behaviour	Verdrängung, Unterdrückung
suburban commuter [səb'ə:bən kə'mju:tə]	someone living in the suburb and working in town	Vorstadtpendler
noose [u:]	loop of rope with a running knot that becomes tighter when the rope is pulled	Schlinge
constriction [kən'strikʃən]	making tight or smaller; the feeling of being shut in	Einschnürung, Beengtheit

to convey s. th. to s. b.	to make known ideas, views etc. to s. b.	jmd etwas mitteilen, etwas vermitteln
coda ['kəudə]	passage, often elaborate in style, that completes a piece of music; here: figuratively applied to the last scenes of an act	Koda, Schlußteil
tart sl	girl or woman of immoral character	'Nutte', Hure
to have frets about s. th.	to be worried or discontented about	sich über etwas ärgern, Bedenken haben
farce-comedy ['fɑːs'kɔmədi]	a comedy full of ridiculous situations intended to make people laugh	possenhafte Komödie
Grand Guignol (French) [grã gin'jɔl]	a person who is involuntarily funny	Kasper, Spaßmacher
to change gear ['giə]	in speeding up or slowing down a car one has to change the gears	einen anderen Gang einlegen, die Gänge wechseln
shift of emphasis ['emfəsis]	change of importance	Verlagerung der Wichtigkeit, des Nachdrucks

p. 13

stagecraft [' – –]	skill or experience in writing plays or directing them	Bühnenkunst, Bühnenerfahrung
light-weightedness	here: being of little importance	'Leichtgewichtigkeit'
pat [æ]	too neat; satisfactory, needing no change	parat; 'fix und fertig'

repercussion [ripəˈkʌʃən]	echoing sound; far-reaching effect	Widerhall; Nach-, Rückwirkungen
a clinging ambiguity [ˌæmbiˈgjuiti]	some doubtful passages that defy interpretation	eine bleibende Unsicherheit, Mehrdeutigkeit
to pin s. th. on s. b.	to classify s. b. for good	jmd ein Etikett anhängen, anheften
sophisticated [səˈfistiˌkeitid]	here: refined, complex, subtle	intellektuell, verfeinert, kultiviert
to have the knack of [næk]	to have the talent, the gift of	die Begabung, das Talent besitzen
sloppy	not done with care and thoroughness	schlampig, nachlässig
cross-talk (pattern)	rapid exchange of remarks	Austausch von Schlagfertigkeiten
vaudeville [ˈvɔdəvil, ˈvəudəvil]	entertainment consisting of singing, dancing, short plays	Variété, Singspiel
to tote Am sl	to carry s. th.	bei sich führen, mit sich schleppen
viable for [ˈvaiəbl]	able to exist without outside help	lebensfähig
triple-bill	a theatre poster consisting of three parts	dreiteiliges Theaterplakat
miniature [ˈminitʃə, ˈminjetʃə]	small-scale copy or model of any object	Miniatur(ausgabe)
asset [ˈæset]	valuable or useful quality	Aktivposten: Vorteil, Vorzug

p. 14

narrative fleetness ['nærətiv, 'fli:tnis]	telling the story in a lively and quick-moving way	erzählerisches Tempo
subtle ['sʌtl]	difficult to perceive; ingenious	fein; heikel, schwierig
futility [fju'tiliti]	state or action of no use or result	Nutzlosigkeit, Vergeblichkeit
decrescendo [ˌdikri'ʃendəu]	(in music) the gradual diminishing of sound	Decrescendo, Nachlassen der Lautstärke
fervent ['fə:vənt]	hot, flowing; showing warmth of feeling	feuerig, glühend; leidenschaftlich
Chekov, Anton Pavlovich ['tʃekɔv]	(1860–1904) Russian dramatist and short-story writer	
Chekhovian [tʃe'kəuviən]	derived from Chekov	Tschechovscher …
to dull	to make monotonous or uninteresting	abstumpfen, trüben
perception [pə'sepʃən]	process by which we become aware of s. th., esp. through the eyes or the mind	(sinnliche, geistige) Wahrnehmung
unflagging	not showing signs of weariness	unermüdlich, unentwegt
pathos ['peiθɔs]	quality in speech or writing which arouses a feeling of pity and sympathy	Pathos, Mitleid, Ergriffensein

miniaturist ['minitʃə,rist]	a painter of miniatures	Miniaturist
skin-grafting	piece of skin of a living person transplanted on another person	Hauttransplantation, Hautübertragung
to lasso [læ'su:]	to catch with a lasso; here: to make s. th. forcibly fit into a context	mit dem Lasso fangen; gewaltsam 'einpassen'
albeit [ɔ:l'bi:it]	obsolete for: although	obgleich, obwohl
to meet s. b.'s requirements	do what s. b. wants done	jem. Anforderungen entsprechen
rectitude ['rekti'tju:d]	upright and straightforward behaviour	Rechtschaffenheit
self-righteousness ['self,raitjəsnis]	conviction of one's own goodness, and that one is better than the others	Selbstgefälligkeit, Selbstgerechtigkeit

p. 15

malicious [mə'liʃəs]	desirous to harm others	boshaft, böswillig
we cannot abide the question	we cannot stand the question	wir können die Frage nicht ertragen
to disentangle [..'tæŋgl]	to make free from complication or confusion	lösen, befreien
to make/hold a brief for	to make an argument in support or favour of	eine Lanze brechen für
racism ['reisizm]	antagonism between different races; belief that one's own race is superior	Rassismus; Rassenpolitik

to be tarred with the same brush	to have the same faults	die gleichen Fehler haben
impartiality [im,pɑ:ʃi'æliti]	the quality of not favouring one more than the other	Unvoreingenommenheit, Unparteilichkeit
to preclude [pri'klu:d]	to prevent, to make impossible	ausschließen
to plump for	to vote for, to choose with confidence	rückhaltlos unterstützen, seine ungeteilte Stimme geben
perfunctory [pə'fʌŋktəri]	done as a duty or routine, but without care or interest	oberflächlich, nachlässig
Arden, John	(born 1930) English dramatist; best known for "Sergeant Musgrave's Dance"	
arbiter ['ɑ:bitə]	= arbitrator: person appointed by two parties to settle a dispute	Schiedsrichter, Schiedsmann
to present an iussue ['isju:]	to present a question that rises for discussion	ein Problem/eine Frage aufwerfen
to subscribe to s. th.	here: to agree with; to share opinion	etwas unterschreiben; zustimmen
to supply evidence	to give or show proof of	den Beweis erbringen
to glut	to supply in excess of demand	übersättigen, überladen

p. 16

boon [u:]	request, favour, advantage	Wohltat, Segen, Gefälligkeit
to glean s. th. from	to gather in small quantities	zus.-lesen, zus.-suchen
conflicting accounts	reports that are contradictory	widersprechende Berichte
persuasive [pə'sweisiv]	able to persuade, convincing	überzeugend
counter-argument	an argument against another	Gegenargument
distortion [dis'tɔ:ʃən]	a false account of; a twist out of the truth	Verzerrung, Verdrehung, Entstellung
to muster s. th. up	to call, collect, or gather together	sammeln, aufbringen
to doom s. b.	to condemn s. b.	jmd verurteilen
a peg for s. th.	here: a pretext, an excuse for a discussion	Aufhänger für; Vorwand, Anlaß
crackling good drama	a good play full of tension and suspense	ein (vor Spannung) knisterndes gutes Drama
to put into a larger perspective	to show the relation between the different aspects more clearly	in einen größeren Zusammenhang stellen
symptomatic of	showing certain signs of	symptomatisch für
Artaud, Antonin [ar'to]	(1896–1948) French poet and essayist who had a large influence on modern drama	

the Renaissance [ri'neisəns]	period of revival of art and literature in Europe in the 14th, 15th, and 16th centuries, based on ancient learning	die Renaissance
Jacobean age [ˌdʒækəu'biːən]	the reign of James I (1603–1925) of England	das Zeitalter Jakobs I.
a new theatre-aesthetic [iːs'θetik]	a new taste by which plays are appreciated	ein neuer Theater-Geschmack
synonymous with [si'nɔniməs]	having the same meaning	gleichbedeutend mit
rigour ['rigə]	sternness, strictness	Strenge
the scores [skɔːz]	copies indicating the music for the different instruments	die Partituren
script	text book, scenario	Textbuch, Drehbuch
replica ['replikə]	exact copy of a work of art	Abdruck, Abklatsch

p. 17

chagrin ['ʃægrin, Am: ʃə'griːn]	feeling of disappointment and irritation	Kummer, Verdruß

Edward Albee

THE AMERICAN DREAM

p. 21 PREFACE

Messrs. = Messieurs ['mesəz]	used as the plural of Mr before a list of men's names: Messrs Miller, Smith, and Markby	die Herren (Müller, Schmidt und Markby)
to be representative of	to represent	verkörpern, darstellen
to tout opinions colloq [taut]	to collect opinions	Meinungen sammeln
antagonistic [æn,tægə'nistik]	adverse, opposed, contrary	gegnerisch, feindlich
playwright ['pleirait]	writer of plays	Bühnenautor, Dramatiker
to last s. b. a lifetime	to be sufficient for a whole life	jmd für ein ganzes Leben reichen
masochist ['mæzəkist]	a man getting pleasure from inflicting cruelties to himself	Masochist, Selbstquäler
foolhardy ['fu:l ...]	foolishly bold, taking unnecessary risks	tollkühn, verwegen
tabloid ['tæb ...]	newspaper with many pictures, and with its news presented in sensational form	Bildzeitung, Sensationsblatt

to offend s. b.'s sensibilities	to hurt the feelings of s. b.	jmd Zartgefühl verletzen
Intellectualist Weekly Sheets	weekly magazines with the news conceived for intellectual readers	intellektuelle Wochenblätter
to go to pieces	to come undone; to break down	in Stücke gehen, zus.-brechen
to submit [səb'mit]	to put forward for opinion or discussion	zu bedenken geben; ergebenst bemerken
arbiter ['ɑːbitə]	person who is to decide the quarrel between two parties	Schiedsrichter
arbiter of morality	one who judges the morals of his fellowmen	Sittenrichter
guardian ['gɑːdiən]	person responsible for a young or incapable person and his property	Hüter, Wächter, Vormund
substitution [,sʌbsti'tjuːʃən]	the act of putting a person or thing in place of another	Unterschiebung; ersatzweise Verwendung
complacency [kəm'pleisənsi]	self-satisfaction; quiet contentment	Zufriedenheit, Selbstgefälligkeit
emasculation [i,mæskju'leiʃən]	quality of being weak and/or effeminate	Entmannung, Verweichlichung
vacuity [væ'kjuːiti]	absence of thought or intelligence	(geistige) Leere, Hohlheit
to take a stand against s. th.	be opposed to; fight against	gegen etwas eintreten
fiction ['fikʃən]	here: s. th. invented or imagined	Fiktion, Märchen

peachy [i:] Am sl	a) like a peach; b) first-rate, grand	pfirsichartig; toll, prima, scharfsinnig
keen	here: of sharp intellect	scharsinnig

p. 22

offensive [ə'fensiv]	causing offence to the mind or senses; disagreeable	anstößig, ärgerniserregend
nihilist ['naiilist]	someone who rejects the current religious and moral beliefs	Nihilist
defeatist [di'fi:tist]	believer in the fact that all our efforts will come to nothing and are of no use	Defätist, Miesmacher; defätistisch
yowl [jaul]	howl, wail	Gejaule, Geheule
to transcend [træn'send]	to go beyond or outside the range of human experience	überschreiten, übersteigen
anguish ['æŋgwiʃ]	severe suffering, esp of the mind	Qual, Pein, Schmerz

p. 23

Mommy ['mʌmi] Am colloq	form for mother, B. E.: mummy	Mammi, Mutti

p. 25

diagonal [dai'ægənəl]	across	diagonal, über Kreuz
rear wall ['ri:ə]	wall at the back	hintere Wand

far stage right	in the background of the right hand side of the stage	auf der rechten hinteren Bühne
archway ['ɑ:tʃwei]	curved structure built as an ornament or gateway	Bogengang, überwölbter Torweg
what can be keeping them?	what can have delayed their arrival?	was kann sie wohl aufhalten?
it never fails	this will always happen	das passiert immer
lease [li:s]	legal agreement by which the owner of land or a building agrees to let another have it for a certain time	Mietvertrag, Pachtvertrag
in advance	beforehand	im voraus
security [si'kjuəriti]	s. th. valuable given as a pledge for the fulfilment of a promise	Kaution, Sicherheit, Bürgschaft
one month's security	the rent for one month as such a pledge	eine Monatsmiete als Sicherheit
reference ['ref ...]	statement about a person's character or abilities	Referenz, Empfehlung, Zeugnis
to check one's references	to examine the correctness of such statements	die Referenzen überprüfen
icebox Am to fix s. th. Am	B. E.: refrigerator B. E.: to repair s. th.	Kühlschrank reparieren
leak [i:]	a hole or crack through which a liquid may wrongly get out	undichte Stelle, Leck
johnny ['dʒɔni] Am sl	toilet, lavatory; here: the toilet pan	Klo; Kloschüssel
you can get away with anything these days	today you can do anything without being punished for it	heute kann man sich alles erlauben

p. 26

beige [beiʒ]	nearly the colour of sand	beige, sandfarben
spang colloq	at once, straightaway	peng, bums
to run into s. b.	meet s. b. quite unexpectedly	jmd in die Arme laufen
wheat-coloured ['wi:t ..]	the colour of wheat	weizenfarben
they put one over on you	they have cheated you	die haben dich reingelegt
adorable [ə'dɔ:rəbl]	loveable, delightful	anbetungswürdig, allerliebst
wheel-chair	a chair for disabled persons that cannot move their legs	Rollstuhl
artificial light [ˌɑ:ti'fiʃəl]	electric light, no daylight	künstliche Beleuchtung
to snap to	here: to answer suddenly just to show that one has been listening	zuschnappen; hier: hervorstoßen
good for you! Am colloq	very good, fine	prima! fein!
to keep right on doing	carry on doing	weitermachen, nicht aufhören
lo and behold! [ləu]	old use, here ironic: look! see!	sieh da!
to clear one's throat	by coughing, for example	sich räuspern
you can't get satisfaction	you are always frustrated and disappointed	man findet keine Befriedigung mehr

p. 28

to get feeble-headed	to lose the correct use of one's mind	geistesschwach werden
her johnny-do's	her evacuation of her bowels	ihr Stuhlgang
to be loaded down with	carrying too many and too heavy parcels	mit etwas überladen sein
look at you!	exclamation to draw s. b.'s attention to his or her own disorderly appearance	schau dich mal an!
to dump down	to put or throw down carelessly	hinfallen lassen, hinwerfen

p. 29

I deserve being talked to that way	mild reproach to tell s. b. that he ought not to speak to one as he does	ich verdiene wohl diese Sprache
to freeze to death	to die from cold	erfrieren
contrite [kən'trait]	showing sorrow for one's own wrongdoing	zerknirscht
to be doomed	to be certain be be lost; to be condemned	verloren sein; dem Untergang geweiht sein
book club	organization selling books to its members at lower prices than ordinary bookshops	Bücherbund, Buchgesellschaft
selection	choice made of s. th.	Auswahl, Auslese
you gotta do Am	you got to do	

to snap at s. b. colloq	shout at s. b.	jemand anfahren, anschnauzen

p. 30

generous ['dʒenərəs]	noble-minded; ready to give freely	großzügig; freigebig
deceitful [di'si:tful]	trying to cheat people; misleading	hinterlistig, falsch; betrügerisch
nursing home	here: home for the aged	Altersheim; B. E.: Privatklinik
to earn one's keep	to earn one's living	seinen Unterhalt verdienen
you can't live off people	you cannot have other people pay for your living	man kann fremden Leuten nicht auf der Tasche liegen

p. 31

get on top of me and bump your uglies vulg.	have sexual intercourse with me	auf mir rumrammeln
to whimper ['(h)wimpə]	to utter weak complaing or frightened sounds as a dog for example	wimmern, winseln
to belch	to send out gas from the stomach noisily through the mouth	rülpsen
rumbling sounds	deep, heavy, continuous sounds	knurrendes Geräusch
homily ['hɔmili]	sermon; long and tedious moralizing talk	Kanzelrede; Predigt

p. 32

tramp	person who goes from place to place and has no regular work; here: a prostitute	Landstreicher; 'Luder', leichtes Mädchen
trollop ['trɔləp]	slatternly woman, mostly of bad character	Schlampe, Luder, Hure
trull	prostitute	Hure
allowance [ə'lauəns]	permission; sum of money allowed to s. o. regulary	Erlaubnis; ausgesetzte Summe; regelmäßig gewährter Geldbetrag
to make allowances for	to consider s. b.'s shortcomings favourably	Zugeständnisse machen
fur [ə:]	hairy skin of animals	Pelz
to get fresh	to become cheeky; show one's bad manners	frech werden

p. 33

colitis [kɔ'laitis]	illness of the bowels	Dickdarmkatarrh
lavender ['lævəndə]	a Mediterranean plant used to perfume linen	Lavendel
van people	the people arriving with the van	die Leute vom Lieferwagen
to cart off	to carry away on a cart	weg-, fortkarren

p. 34

masculine ['mæskjulin]	belonging to the male sex	männlich

it hurts the gums	it hurts the flesh round the teeth	es tut am Zahnfleisch weh
jelly ['dʒeli]	clear, soft, transparent food substance made from gelatine or from fruit juice and sugar	Gallert, Sülze; Gelee; schwabbelige Masse
to turn into jelly	to be scared stiff; to get the 'funk'	'Schiß' kriegen
indecisive [ˌindi'saisiv]	not knowing what to decide	unschlüssig, unentschlossen

p. 35

don't be rude!	don't be impolite!	sei nicht unhöflich! sei nicht unverschämt!
I don't mind if I do colloq	I'd like to	gerne; mit Vergnügen
to dodder	to walk or move in a shaky way; to jabber	vor Schwäche zittern; 'quasseln'
efficient [i'fiʃənt]	able to perform duties well; thorough	tüchtig; gründlich
to recall s. th.	remember s. th.	sich an etwas erinnern
to scold s. o.	give s. o. a piece of one's mind	jmd (aus)schelten

p. 36

unattractive [ˌʌnə'træktiv]	without any appeal, not pleasing	reizlos, unattraktiv
in the swing	in a boat-shaped device held by ropes or chains	in der Luftschaukel

hem	border or edge of cloth	Kleidersaum, Rand
slip	woman's undergarment	Unterkleid, Unterrock

p. 37

he went sticky wet	allusion to the fact that he had a sexual ejaculation	er wurde klebrig feucht
he is a caution ['kɔ:ʃən]	he causes amusement by his conversation or by what he does	er ist eine ulkige Nummer
to have one's finger in the pie	to be concerned in the matter	seine Hand im Spiel haben, 'mitmischen'
activities (mostly pl)	occupations in one's spare time	Freizeitgestaltung; Freizeitbeschäftigung

p. 38

misgiving	feeling of doubt, suspicion, mistrust	böse Ahnung, Befürchtung
qualm [kwɑ:m, kwɔ:m]	feeling of doubt; temporary feeling of sickness	Skrupel, Bedenken; Übelkeit
stitch	the passing of a needle in and out of cloth	Stich
to dry up colloq Am	to hold one's tongue, to stop talking	die 'Klappe' halten
fluid ['flu:id]	liquid substance, such a water	(physiologische) Flüssigkeit, Körpersaft

to cake	to become coated with s. th. that becomes hard when dry	verkrusten, zus.-backen
spine [ai]	backbone	Rückgrat, Wirbelsäule
to complain about/of	to say that one is not satisfied with	sich beklagen
gnarled [nɑ:ld]	twisted and rough, covered with knobs	knorrig (vom Baum)
to sag	to hang down unevenly, to hang sideways	schlaff werden, nachlassen
to twist	to turn or wind around the other	(ver)drehen, winden
twisted into the shape of a complaint	a highly original metaphorical expression of Albee's	wie wenn man sie in die Form einer Beanstandung verdreht hätte

p. 39

ambition [æm'biʃən]	strong desire to get on in life	Ehrgeiz, Streben
that's the ticket! Am colloq	that's just the right thing!	das ist genau das Richtige
deprecating ['depri, ...]	feeling and expressing disapproval	mißbilligend, ablehnend
village idiot	someone who is made fun of	Dorftrottel
stickler	a pedant; one who insists on the importance of formality	Kleinigkeitskrämer, Pedant
exponent [iks'pəunənt]	a person that is a good example of	Repräsentant

to write s. th. up	to describe in full detail	ausführlich darstellen, eingehend berichten
psychiatric [ˌsaikiˈætrik]	having to do with diseases of the mind	psychiatrisch
journal [ˈdʒəːnəl]	a periodical	Fachzeitschrift
nuts colloq	nonsense	Quatsch, Blödsinn
she's rural [ˈruːrəl]	she is not refined; she has bad manners	sie kommt vom Lande

p. 40

I can pull that stuff as easily as you can	I can talk in that way as easily as you can	ich kann das Zeug ebenso leicht herunterleiern wie du
the age of deformity [diˈfɔːmiti]	ironic: our age prefers to deform things rather than leave them natural	das Zeitalter der Verunstaltung
rhythm [ˈriðəm]	regular succession of weak and strong stresses	Takt, Rhytmus
content [kənˈtent]	satisfaction	Zufriedenheit, Befriedigung
can I say my piece?	may I speak my mind now?	darf ich sagen, was ich auf dem Herzen habe?
to jabber away [ˈdʒæbə]	to talk in what seems a rapid and confused manner	drauflosquasseln, drauflosquatschen
snippety [ˈsnipiti]	snippy; pert; 'sniffy' 'snooty'	schroff; barsch, schnippisch

4 Ludwig, New American Drama

p. 41

enema bottle ['enimə]	syringe for an injection into the rectum	Klistierspritze, Einlauf
Pekinese [ˌpiːkiˈniːz]	special breed of dogs	Pekinese (Hunderasse)
stock	special breed; race	Rasse, Menschenschlag
delivery [diˈlivəri]	childbirth, confinement	Entbindung
yup = yep [jep]	Am popular expression for 'yes'	
nope [nəup]	Am popular expression for 'no'	
hedgehog ['hedʒhɔg]	insect eating animal, covered with spines; fig. s. o. whom it is not pleasant to disagree with	Igel; Am Stachelschwein
to stick up for s. b.	to come to s. b.'s defence, help s. b.	jmd Beistand leisten
kid Am sl	child; young person	Kind; junger Mensch
the kid is all mixed up	the child is quite confused	das Kind ist ganz durcheinander

p. 42

tube [tjuːb]	long hollow cylinder of metal, rubber, glass or plastic	Röhre, Röhrchen, Gummischlauch
tract	here: part of the bowels	anatomischer Trakt; Verdauungssystem

Responsible Citizen Activity	working for one's community, mostly without pay	Betätigung als verantwortlicher Bürger, Ehrenamt
to indulge in activities	to have various occupations	Betätigungen nachgehen
Fulbright Scholarship:	Senator Fulbright initiated in 1946 a Congressional Act that provided for a large part of the proceeds from the sale of US war surplus property in foreign countries to be used to finance the mutual exchange of students, teachers, and other cultural workers	
Guggenheim Fellowship:	a foundation, as in a college or university, the income of which is bestowed upon a student to aid him persuing further studies	
Guggenheim	US industrialist and philanthropist (1836–1939)	
to shoot the works	Am colloq: to go all out; to risk all	alles auf eine Karte setzen
Prix de Rome	certainly an ironic allusion to some international prize	
air raid	airborne attack	Luftangriff
Ladies' Auxiliary Air Raid Committee	humoristically modelled on Women's Auxiliary Air Force (WAAF)	Damenluftschutzhilfskommitee
badger ['bædʒə]	small, grey-white animal living in holes	Dachs
to badger s. b.	to worry or tease or bother s. b.	hetzen, plagen, belästigen
surfeit ['sə:fit]	too much of anything	Übermaß, Überdruß, Ekel

p. 43

a run on s.b./s.th.	everyone trying to be the first to arrive so as to get hold of the person or thing desired	ein Wettlauf um/ eine Jagd auf jmd/etw
adult ['ædʌlt, ə'dʌlt]	grown-up	erwachsen, Erwachsener
argumentative [ɑ:gju'mentətiv]	fond of arguing, full of arguments	streitlustig, strittig, umstritten
to mortify ['mɔ:tifai]	to humiliate; to make ashamed	demütigen, kränken
girl talk	things that girls talk about	Mädchengeschwätz
to feel faint	to feel weak, exhausted	sich matt fühlen, einer Ohnmacht nahe sein

p. 44

to quit [kwit]	to stop doing; to go away; to leave	aufhören; weggehen; ausziehen
a false sense of security [si'kjuəriti]	the feeling that one is safe, when in reality one is not safe	ein falsches Gefühl der Sicherheit
to tend s. o.	lit.: to watch over, attend to; here: to pick a bone with s. b.	sich um jmd kümmern; hier: mit jmd abrechnen
I'll fix you sl	I'll get even with you	ich werd dir's heimzahlen
go soak your head!	the devil take you!	scher dich zum Teufel!
dearie ['diəri]	endearment for: dear	Liebchen

simile ['simili]	comparison of one thing to another	Gleichnis
to implore [im'plɔ:]	to request earnestly, to beg	anflehen, beschwören

p. 45

to beseech s.b. [i :]	to request earnestly, to beg	jmd anflehen
muddle-headed	not clear-thinking, confused	konfus, wirrköpfig
yours truly	humorous allusion to oneself	meine Wenigkeit
volunteer capacity [ˌvɔlən'tiə kə'pæsiti]	what can be done by people working from their own free will and without pay	Leistungsfähigkeit von Freiwilligen
Bye-Bye Adoption Service	ironically meant, as adoption does not imply leave-taking	der Adoptionsdienst 'Lebewohl'
deaf [def]	not being able to hear	taub
enthralling [in'θrɔ:liŋ]	thrilling, charming	fesselnd; bezaubernd
to bite one's fingers	to nibble at one's fingernails, mostly from nervousness	die Fingernägel kauen

p. 46

to be blessed with [blest]	to be fortunate in having	gesegnet sein mit
blessed ['blesid]	holy, sacred	gesegnet, selig (Adj.!)
a bumble of joy	an association of bundle, bumble, bungle	ein Freuden-'bümbel'

bumble	some conceited overbearing civil servant	kleiner aufgeblasener Beamter
to bungle	to spoil	verpfuschen, verpatzen
bundle	several things packed together	Bündel
engrossing [enˈgrəusiŋ]	taking up all one's attention and interest	fesselnd, spannend
to take heart	to pluck up courage	sich ein Herz fassen
irrelevant [iˈrelivənt]	being of no importance	unerheblich, belanglos
hot stuff colloq	things that 'turn s. b. on' sexually	'heißes' Zeug
to have a penchant for [pãˈʃã; Am: ˈpenˈtʃənt]	to have a liking or inclination for	Hang zu, Neigung, Vorliebe für etw. haben
pornography [pɔːˈnɔgrəfi]	pictures or texts intended to arouse sexual desire	Pornographie, Schmutz
whoopee [ˈhuːˈpiː]	orgy	Orgie: Sauf- oder Sexparty
whoopee!	exclamation of joy	juchhu!
that is beside the point	that is not relevant to the point in question	das gehört nicht zur Sache
gripping	interesting, captivating	fesselnd, packend

p. 47

to be taken places	to be taken along in a car and shown places	wohin mitgenommen werden
to be put places	to be loged somewhere	wohin 'gesteckt' werden

that was enough of a blow	that was quite a shock	das war ein ziemlich harter Schlag
to gouge out ['gaudʒ'aut]	to press out with force, esp. with the thumbs	herauspressen, herausdrücken
disgusting	causing a strong feeling of dislike or distaste	ekelhaft, ekelerregend
you-know-what	euphemism for penis	'Pillermann', 'Dingsda'
resentful against [ri'zentfəl]	feeling angry and bitter at s. th.	aufgebracht, ärgerlich
to call s. b. a dirty name	use abusive language, insult s. b.	jemanden gemein beschimpfen
to have guts	literally: to have bowels; figuratively: to have courage	Eingeweide haben; Mut haben
spineless ['spainlis]	without a backbone; without determination	ohne Rückgrat
clay	sticky earth that becomes hard when baked	Lehm

p. 48

the last straw	the last hope one has to cling to	der letzte Strohhalm, an den man sich klammert
it up and died	it got out of bed and died	es stand auf und starb
them apples	vulgar for: those apples	
trouble-maker	one who always causes troubles	Unruhestifter
to restrain s. b.	to hold s. b. back, to keep him under control	jmd zurückhalten

p. 49

smug [ʌ]	self-satisfied altough there is nothing to be proud of	selbstgefällig, blasiert
no sense of proportion	no insight into and no understanding of reality	keinen Sinn für die wahren Größenordnungen haben
to relate s. th. to	to connect things in thought and meaning	etw in Zusammenhang bringen mit

p. 50

to mull (over) s. th.	to ponder over, to reflect on s. th.	über etw nachgrübeln, nachdenken
spry adj. Am	lively, nimble	flink, lebhaft, munter
Lordy!	exclamation for 'Good God'	mein Gottchen!
to look chipper Am	to look cheerful, smart	'aufgekratzt', munter aussehen
I could go for you	I would immediately fall in love with you	ich könnte wild nach dir werden
to flex one's muscles	bend one's arm so as to show one's muscles	die Muskeln spielen lassen
gym [dʒim]	short für gymnasium	Turnhalle

p. 51

to be in the movies	be a film star	Filmschauspieler sein
to insult [in'sʌlt]	offend	beleidigen

to be insultingly good-looking	to be so good-looking that it offends one's sense of decency	unverschämt gut aussehen
profile ['prəufail]	side-view, esp. of the face	Profil
gibberish ['dʒibəriʃ, also: 'gi..]	unintelligible talk	dummes Geschwätz, Quatsch, Kauderwelsch
folks Am colloq	familiar address of people one does not know	Leute (als Anrede)
honey ['hʌni] Am	dearie, sweetie	etwa: Schätzchen

p. 52

I can sense these things	I can feel these things instinctively	ich fühle diese Dinge
quandary ['kwɔndəri]	difficulty; state of doubt and perplexity	Verlegenheit, Schwierigkeit
to be in a quandary	to be in a scrape	in der Klemme sitzen
to run a baking contest	to organize a baking competition	einen Backwettbewerb veranstalten
barn [ɑ:]	covered building for storing hay, grains etc.	Scheune

p. 53

nom de boulangère (French) [nɔ̃ də bulãʒɛ:r]	humorous allusion to 'nom de plume': a pen name, a writer's assumed name	Künstlername, den sich ein Bäcker zulegt.

store-bought cake	a cake bought at the baker's; a ready-made cake	im Laden gekaufter Kuchen
to slip s. th. in	to smuggle s. th. in	dazwischenmogeln, unbemerkt einschleusen
unbeknownst [ˌʌnbi'nəunst]	humorous: without anybody having the slightest idea	völlig unerkannt
resourceful [ri'sɔ:sful]	good and quick in finding means and ways to solve problems	einfallsreich, erfinderisch
pioneer stock [ˌpaiə'niə]	descendants from the American pioneers	'echt vom Schlage der Pioniere'
smackerolas sl [ˌsmækə'rəulɑ:z]	diminutive for 'smacker' (sl), meaning 'dollar'	Dollarchen
loggerhead ['lɔgəhed]	a silly, stupid person	Dummkopf, Schafskopf
to do some modelling ['mɔdəliŋ]	to sit as a model to a painter or sculptor	ein bißchen Modell stehen
nosy ['nəuzi] colloq	curious, inquisitive	neugierig
to compensate ['kɔmpən,seit]	to make good, to make a suitabel payment	kompensieren, ausgleichen, wettmachen

p. 54

perception [pə'sepʃən]	process by which we become aware of things, esp through the sense of sight or the power of the mind	sinnliche und geistige Wahrnehmung

placenta [pləˈsentə]	organ by which the foetus is nourished	Mutterkuchen, Nachgeburt
fraternal [frəˈtəːnəl]	brotherly	brüderlich
identical twins [aiˈdentikəl]	twins from one single fertilized ovum	eineiige Zwillinge
ovum, pl. ova [ˈəuvəm, ˈəuvə]	female germ or sex cell	Eizelle, Ovum
kinship	relationship by blood	(Bluts-)Verwandtschaft
temple	flat part of either side of the head between the forehead and the ear	Schläfe
departure of innocence	loss of innocence	Verlust der Unschuld
numb [nʌm]	without feeling, stiff (with cold)	ohne Empfindung, gefühllos, abgestumpft
groin	depression between the stomach and the thigh	(anat.) Leistengegend, Leiste
agony [ˈægəni]	great pain or suffering (of mind or body)	Höllenqual, Todeskampf; heftiger Schmerz

p. 55

to drain	to lead off by means of drains or pipes	Flüssigkeit abfließen lassen, hier: austrocknen lassen
to tear asunder [əˈsʌndə]	to pull into two parts	auseinanderreißen

to disembowel [ˌdisim'bauəl]	to cut out the bowels of an animal	die Eingeweide herausnehmen, auswaiden
I accept the syntax around me ['sintæks]	I imitate the language that I hear spoken around me	ich übernehme den um mich her gesprochenen Satzbau
to bow one's head [bau]	to bend one's head (as a sign of greeting or respect)	den Kopf neigen
acquiescence [ˌækwi'esəns]	silent acceptance or silent consent	Einwilligung, Duldung
I've got to go into my act	I've got to do my job now	ich muß jetzt in die 'Sache einsteigen'
double-take	being slow in understanding	'Spätzündung'

p. 56

to shrug one's shoulders	to raise and lower one's shoulders in order to express resignation	mit den Achseln zucken
it figures Am sl	it is obvious; it is evident	das versteht sich; es ist klar
to meddle with	busy oneself without being asked	sich einmischen
brief [iː]	short	kurz
in disbelief	not believing	ungläubig

p. 57

to take s. th. in	consider a situation carefully	die Lage überschauen, genau betrachten

to garble s. th.	to make a false or incomplete selection of facts	(einen Text) entstellen, verstümmeln
to accummulate [əˈkjuːmjuˌleit]	to heep up	ansammeln, ananhäufen

p. 58

what with delays and all	because of all these delays	mit all den Verzögerungen und so
to be relieved [iː]	to feel that one's anxiety and distress have been taken away	sich erleichtert fühlen
to dim the lights	to make the lights shine less brightly	abblenden
to tiptoe [ˈtiptəu]	to walk on the top of one's toes	auf Zehenspitzen gehen
to be framed	a picture is framed in	eingerahmt sein
to sniffle	to make sounds as if the nose is partly stopped up	heulen, schniefen
to urge s. o. to cheerfulness	to cheer s. b. up, to encourage s. b.	jmd aufmuntern

p. 59

to poke s. b. (in the ribs)	to push s. b. violently with one's elbows	jmd einen Rippenstoß geben
sirree [ˌsəːˈriː] Am colloq	used in contempt or annoyance often in the sense of 'of course'	etwa: aber klar
sauterne [soˈtəːn]	originally applying to a sweet, white French wine; in USA: any sweet white wine	süßer französischer Weißwein; USA: süßer Weißwein

top-notch colloq	first class	prima, erstklassig
to straighten out	to smooth out; to arrange things	'ausbügeln', in Ordnung bringen

p. 60

fuzzy ['fʌzi]	blurred; indistinct in shape or outline	benommen, benebelt
to sidle up to s. o.	to walk up to s. o. in a shy or nervous way	sich an jmd heranmachen
that wraps it up! [ræps] Am sl	that brings it to an end	Das wär's!

JACK RICHARDSON

GALLOWS HUMOUR PART ONE

p. 63

illusive [i'lu:siv; i'lju:..]	deceptive; based on illusion	trügerisch, illusorisch
arcane [ɑ:'kein]	secret; hidden	geheimnisvoll, verborgen
stern [ə:]	strict, severe; resolute	streng, hart; unnachgiebig
dictum, pl. dicta/ dictums ['diktəm, pl.: 'diktə]	formal expression of opinion; saying	Ausspruch, Maxime; geflügeltes Wort
to chortle [tʃɔ:tl]	to give a loud chuckle of glee	glucksen; frohlocken

aesthetics [ˌes'θetiks]	science that tries to make clear the laws and principles of beauty	Ästhetik (= Lehre vom Schönen)
to push past enjoyment to criticism		am Vergnügen vorbeigehen und zur Kritik kommen
to hyphenate ['haifə,neit]	to join words with a hyphen	Wörter mit einem Bindestrich schreiben
capricious [kə'priʃəs]	often changing, guided by caprice; unreliable	launenhaft, launisch
semantic laxity [si'mæntik 'læksiti]	being imprecise and inattentive in the proper use of words	ungenaue Verwendung von Ausdrücken
perfunctory [pə:'fʌŋktəri]	done as a duty but without care or interest	oberflächlich, flüchtig, mechanisch
venerable ['ven..]	deserving respect because of age, character, associations	ehrwürdig; verehrungswürdig
to ease s. th. into ..	to move or put in place gradually and with care	vorsichtig einordnen
to tax s. b.	to try s. b.'s nerves, e. g. by talking too much	jmd anstrengen, strapazieren
sobersides ['səubə,saidz]	boring and colourless person	Trauerkloß, fader Kerl
with impunity [im'pju:niti]	getting away with s. th.	ungestraft
to give s. b. the lie	to make him see that ohne realizes that he is lying	jmd lügen strafen
to clock the number of chuckles	to measure the chuckles	die Anzahl der Lacher registrieren

p. 64

flaw [flɔ:]	crack, fault; s. th. that lessens the value of a thing	Fehler, Makel; Mängel
a knotty subject ['nɔti]	one that is difficult to solve	ein kompliziertes Thema
lexicographer [ˌleksi'kɔgrəfə]	person who compiles a dictionary	Lexikograph
provocative [prə'vɔkətiv]	serving to provoke; stimulating	provozierend, herausfordernd
lamentation	expression of grief	Klage, Lamentieren
sub- plot ['sʌb'plɔt]	a plot subordinate to the principle one	Nebenhandlung
relief [ri'li:f]	lessening or ending or removal of pain, stress, anxiety	Erleichterung; Entspannung
vapid ['væpid]	tasteless, uninteresting	schal, seicht; öde, fade
antidote ['ænti,dəut]	medecine used against a poison	Gegengift; Gegenmittel
to numb [nʌm]	to take away, wholly or partially the power of sensation or motion	gefühllos machen
to entangle [in'tæŋgl]	to make complicated and intricate	verwickeln, verwirren
Stagirite ['stædʒi, rait]	inhabitant of Stagira; here: Aristotle	Stagirit (= Aristoteles)
compulsion for purity [kəm'pʌlʃən]	i. e. the Aristotelian demand that a play should be conceived in the unity of time, place and action	

kernel ['kə:nəl]	fig.: the central or important part of a subject or problem	Kern, Wesen; Wesentliches
myopia [mai'əupiə]	shortsightedness	Kurzsichtigkeit
Don Quixote ['dɔn'kwiksət]	hero of a Spanish romance ridiculing knight-errantry, hence a person who is ridiculously chivalrous or romantic with high, but impractical sentiments or aims	Don Quichote
pathetic [pə'θetik]	expressing sadness, arousing pity; touching	pathetisch, rührend, ergreifend
pretension	a claim put forward whether true or false; a bold assertion	Anspruch; pl.: Absichten, Ambitionen
Monsieur Jourdain [məs'jø ʒur'dɛ̃]	main character in Molière's comedy "Le bourgeois Gentilhomme"; he is an upstart whose ambition constantly exposes him to ridicule	
chaotic [kei'ɔtik]	in chaos, i. e. in a state of complete absence of order	chaotisch
hedonism ['hi:də,nizəm]	belief that pleasure is the chief good	Hädonismus (Lehre von der Lustempfindung)
a perceptive reader [pə'septiv]	one who quickly and easily understands the author's intentions	ein scharfsinniger Leser
to tickle and bustle s. o. into laughter	to make s. b. laugh	jmd gewaltsam zum Lachen bringen

to tickle	to excite the nerves of the skin so as to cause laughter	kitzeln
to bustle s. b. into s. th. ['bʌsl]	to move s. b. quickly and excitedly	jmd in etwas hineinhetzen; antreiben
peak [i:]	pointed top, e. g. that of a mountain	Spitze, Gipfel

p. 65

impertinence [im'pə:tinəns]	being impertinent, i. e. not showing proper respect	Unverschämtheit, Ungehörigkeit
Shavian ['ʃeiviən]	of, pertaining to, or like George Bernard Shaw	von Shaw
bluster	violence, noise	Brausen, Toben, Lärmen
palatable ['pæl..]	agreeable to the taste or to the mind	schmackhaft, angenehm
to purge [ə:]	to free s. b. from fear, suspicion; to clear of a charge	befreien, säubern; reinigen
connotation [ˌkɔno'teiʃən]	the different meanings of a word	(Wort)bedeutung, Begriffsinhalt
applicable ['æpli..]	that can be applied to some purpose	anwendbar auf
slapstick ['slæp...] (comedy)	low comedy of the roughest kind	Radau-, Klamaukstück
inadequacy [in'ædikwesi]	insufficiency, shortcoming	Unzulänglichkeit, Unangemessenheit
to stroke	here: to sketch; to outline in a few strokes	umreißen, skizzieren

PROLOGUE

p. 69

to fidget ['fidʒit]	to move the body or part of it about nervously	herumzappeln, nervös sein
to squirm [ə:]	to twist the body, to wriggle (from discomfort, shame)	sich krümmen, sich winden
to sulk	to be in a bad temper and show this by refusing to talk	schmollen, trotzen; schlechter Laune sein
a fit of temper	sudden attack of anger	Wutanfall, .. ausbruch
to salvage ['sælvidʒ]	to rescue; to save from danger	retten
to snip out	to cut out with scissors, esp. in short, quick strokes	herausschnippeln, herausschneiden
diversion [dai'və:ʒən]	diverting; the act of turning s. th. aside or giving it a different direction	Abwechslung; Ablenkung
bonus ['bəunəs] pl.: bonuses	payment in addition to what is necessary or expected	Prämie, Sondervergütung
to relax	to cause or allow to become less tight, stiff, strict or rigid	entspannen; nachlassen
blunt	(of a person or what he says) plain; not troubling to be polite	grob, ungeschliffen; barsch
heavy-handed	awkward, clumsy	ungeschickt, plump

subtlety ['sʌtlti]	the ability to be quick and clever at seeing or making delicate differences; sensitivity	Feinheit, Spitzfindigkeit
wag	merry person, full of amusing sayings and fond of practical jokes	Schalk, Spaßvogel; Witzbold
common denominater [diːˈnɔmiˌneitə]		gemeinsamer Nenner
to skulk along	to hide, move secretly through cowardice, or to avoid work or duty	herumschleichen, lauern; sich herumdrücken
flute [fluːt]	musical wind instrument in the form of a wooden pipe with holes to be stopped by the fingers	Flöte
tabor ['teibə]	small drum, esp. one used to accoumpany a pipe	Tamburin
to clank	make a tinkling or ringing sound	klirren, rasseln

p. 70

alehouse ['eil..]	public house, where beer and ale are sold	Bierschenke
overbusty coll. ['əuvə'bʌsti]	having extraordinarily big breasts	etwa: vollbusig
ingénue French [ɛ̃ʒeny]	a young woman or girl who is innocent and artless	naives Mädchen; Unschuld vom Lande

rapport [ræ'pɔ:(t)]	relationship	Beziehung, Verhältnis
jeer [dʒiə]	speaking or shouting in a mocking, derisive manner	Spott, Hohn, Stichelei
catcall [' – –]	shrill call or whistle in token of impatience or derision	Auspfeifen (als Mißbilligung); schriller Pfiff
to etch	use a needle and acid to make a picture on a metal plate from which copies may be printed	ätzen (Glas, Metall) eingravieren
lascivious [lə'siviəs]	having lustful desires; tending to produce sensual desires	wollüstig, geil; lüstern
to blur s. th.	to make indistinct	verwischen, undeutlich machen
to wiggle	here: to wriggle: move with quick, short, side-to side movements	unruhig hin- und herbewegen
a tardy member ['ta:di]	one that is late, slow, reluctant	langsam, träge, säumig
to make an ass of oneself	to make a fool of o. s.	sich lächerlich machen, sich blamieren
to tug at s. b.	to pull, draw, or drag with effort	heftig ziehen, zerren, reißen

p. 71

beauty salon [sa'lɔ̃; 'sælɔ:ŋ]	an establishment for hairdressing, manicuring cosmetic treatment; auch: beauty parlour	Schönheitssalon, Kosmetiksalon

gallows pl. ['gæləuz]	wooden framework on which to put criminals to death by hanging	Galgen

PART ONE

p. 73

cot	small, easily moved bed	Feldbett; hier: Pritsche
sole ['səul]	single, only	einzig, alleinig
barred into sections [bɑ:d]	barred in a way that square sections are formed	so vergittert, daß sich Quadrate ergeben
platter	large shallow dish for serving food	Servierplatte, Tablett
to deck with s. th.	to decorate, adorn, dress elegantly with s. th.	ausschmücken, dekorieren
Queen Anne dishes	dishes in the style of Queen Anne (1702–1714)	
cover dish	a dish covered with a lid	Schüssel mit Deckel; Terrine
sauceboat ['sɔ:sbəut]	vessel in which sauce is served at table	Saucière, Soßenschüssel
to attire [ə'taiə]	to dress, to put on	sich kleiden
a thin face of angle and bone		ein hageres knochiges Gesicht
indeterminate [,indi'tə:minit]	uncertain; not decided, unsettled	unbestimmt, unsicher

lap	that part of the body below the waist on which, when in a sitting posture, one may conveniently support anything	Schoß
to attend to s. th.	to look after s. th	sich kümmern um; sich befassen mit
fragile ['frædʒail]	easily injured, broken or destroyed	zerbrechlich
inoffensive [,inə'fensiv]	not giving offence, not objectionable, harmless	harmlos, unschädlich
to scribble	to write quickly and carelessly	kritzeln
scribbling	here: the wrinkles and marks that can be seen on his face	etwa: Markierung
to hum	to sing with one's lips closed with a buzzing sound	summen
pitch and volume	degree of highness and fullness and quantitiy of sound	Stimmhöhe und Stimmvolumen

p. 74

to tattoo [tæ'tu:]	to mark s. b.'s skin with permanent designs	tätowieren
in the trade	in the same branch of business	in der Branche
incense ['insens]	substance producing a sweet smell, when burning	Weihrauch, Räucherwerk

beaded curtain ['bi:did]	curtain as used in Mediterranean countries where long strings of beads replace the door during the warm season	Vorhang aus Perlenschnüren
to humanize ['hju:mənaiz]	to make human or humane	vermenschlichen, humanisieren
morsel ['mɔ:səl]	tiny piece of s. th.	Stückchen, (Lecker)bissen
heady ['hedi]	affecting the brain, e. g. alcohol; acting on impulse	berauschend, ungestüm
abominable [ə'bɔminəbl]	causing disgust	abscheulich, ekelhaft
to shuffle	to walk dragging one's feet	mit schlurfenden Schritten gehen
hysterectomy [,histə'rektəmi]	complete removal of the uterus	Hysterektomie (= Totaloperation)
scar [ɑ:]	the mark left on the skin after the healing of a wound	Narbe
scraggly Am	supposedly derived from "scraggy" + "-ly"; unkempt, shaggy	struppelig, zottelig; ungepflegt
a run in the stocking	ladder in the stocking	Laufmasche

p. 75

co-operative [kəu'ɔpərətiv]	willing to help or work together with others	hilfsbereit; zur Mitarbeit bereit
to turn down an appeal	to refuse to reconsider a legal sentence	einen Einspruch ablehnen

to thumb one's nose Am	to cock a snook at s. b.	eine lange Nase drehen
to thumb-nose little phrases at the world	to cause people to laugh unkindly at the world	die Welt in kleinen Sprüchen verhöhnen
to have an axe to grind	to persue one's own advantage or profit	eigennützige Zwecke verfolgen; es auf etw. abgesehen haben
physicist ['fizisist]	student of or specialist in physics	Physiker; Naturforscher
to mope [məup]	to give oneself up to sadness or low spirits	den Kopf hängen lassen, Trübsal blasen
subatomic particles [ˌsʌbə'tɔmik]	particles that are still smaller than an atom	subatomare Teilchen
executioner [ˌeksə'kju:ʃənə]	one who executes a death sentence	Scharfrichter
homicidal [ˌhɔmi'saidəl]	derived from "homicide": the killing of a human being; murder	mörderisch, mordlustig
maniac ['meiniæk]	raving madman	Wahnsinniger
to pep up	to inspire with energy and vigour	aufmöbeln, in Schwung bringen
chef (de cuisine) [ʃɛf də kyi'zin]	a head cook	Küchenchef
to have a little fling	to make merry	ein bißchen auf die Pauke hauen, sich austoben

p. 76

to set s. b. off to advantage	to make s. b. appear at his best	jmd vorteilhaft hervortreten lassen
to set off	to put forward	abheben, kontrastieren
to poke at s. th.	to push or prod at s. th.	an etwas stoßen, puffen, knuffen
copulation [ˌkɔpjuˈleiʃən]	sexual intercourse	Paarung
to prop up	to support or prevent from falling	abstützen, absteifen
effusion (of gratitude) [iˈfju:ʒən]	sentimental demonstration of thankfulness	Erguß von Dankbarkeit
penal [ˈpi:nəl] penal code	liable to punishment a code defining crimes and describing the method and degree of punishment	Straf... Strafgesetzbuch
to take the sting out of s. th.	to calm down, to make less exciting	etw. entschärfen; den Stachel nehmen
sting	sharp defensive or offensive organ of a bee or a wasp	Stachel
capital punishment [ˈkæpitl]	a death sentence; the death penalty for a crime	Todesstrafe
cut and dried	ready for use; prepared by others	fix und fertig; fertig zubereitet
to put people off about s. th.	to dissuade people from doing s. th.	die Leute von etwas abbringen

clack	sharp, short sound of objects struck together	Klappern, Geklapper
cadence ['keidəns]	rhythm in sound; the rise and fall of the voice in speaking	Rhythmus, Takt; Kadenz
cobblestones [' – –]	round smooth stones, formerly used for the paving of streets	Kopfsteinplaster
trite phrases [trait]	used so often as to have become commonplace by repetition	abgedroschene Redensarten; banale Floskeln
spice [spais]	an aromatic, pungent vegetable substance	Gewürz, Würze

p. 77

crust	a hard-baked surface on bread or fried meat	Kruste
seductive [si'dʌktiv]	attractive, alluring	verführerisch
unpremeditated [ˌʌnpri'mediteitid]	not planned or considered beforehand	unbeabsichtigt; nicht vorsätzlich
dash	spirit, vigour; ostentatious display	Schwung, Schmiß; Glanz
cube [kju:b]	a small cell	hier: kleine Zelle
snug	sheltered from wind and cold; cosy	gemütlich, behaglich
tentative ['tentə,tiv]	hesitant, lacking experience and conviction	zögernd, zaghaft
de trop [də'tro] French	superfluous; too many	überflüssig

a preceptorial finger [ˌpriːsepˈtɔːriəl]	the raised forefinger which is to give emphasis to what is said	ein lehrhaft erhobener Zeigefinger

p. 78

a pinched face	a haggard, pale face	ein schmales, abgehärmtes Gesicht
to furrow [ˈfʌrəu]	to make long deep cuts in the ground with a plough; here: to wrinkle	(zer)furchen
pimp	a pander who acts as a go-between in sexual intrigues	Kuppler, Zuhälter
to pimp for s. b.	to hook customers for a prostitute	Kunden für jmd werben; für jmd "anschaffen"
to retrieve s. th.	to get s. th. back; to regain	wiedererlangen, -bekommen
lint Am	a piece of thread, a cotton fibre	Fussel, kleines Fädchen
lapel [ləˈpel]	part of the breast of a coat or jacket folded back and forming the continuation of the collar	Rockaufschlag, Revers
splatter Am	mixture of "spatter" and "splash"	umherspritzen, beschmutzen
That will raise the deuce with my stomach [djuːs, ˈstʌmək]	that will upset my stomach	Das wird mir den Magen umdrehen
to snarl	(of dogs) to utter a sharp, angry growl	wütend knurren; die Zähne fletschen

p. 79

sink	a basin with a drain pipe, where dirty water is drained	Ausguß, Spülstein
to hunch one's shoulders	to bend one's back so as to form a hunch	die Schultern hochziehen, sich zusammenkauern
moon phases ['feiziz]	the periods between the full moon and the new moon	Mondphasen
to butcher ['butʃə]	to slaughter animals; to prepare them for being sold as meat	schlachten
an even dozen [ʌ]	exactly twelve things of a kind	genau ein Dutzend
to pinch s. th. fam.	to steal, to take away illegally	klauen, stehlen
to inch back from	to withdraw very slowly	sich Stück für Stück zurückziehen

p. 80

to compete with [kəm'piːt]	contend with another for a prize or some other advantage	konkurrieren, wetteifern
number - patch	patch sewn onto the jacket of a prisoner with the prison-number on it	Tuchflecken mit der Sträflingsnummer
ledger ['ledʒə]	principal book of accounts of a business establishment	Hauptbuch
it has a nice ring to it	that sounds nice	das klingt nicht schlecht

fussy [ʌ]	excited, fidgety, fretful	aufgeregt, hektisch; hier: kleinlich, pedantisch
to smooth out [smu:ð]	to make calm, to mollify one's feelings	(aus)bügeln, glätten
miniature ['miniətʃə, auch 'minitʃə]	a painting of small dimensions and excellent workmanship	Miniatur-(gemälde), Nachbildung im kleinen
to twitch	move with a quick spasmodic jerk	zucken

p. 81

to clutch [ʌ]	to seize firmly	fassen, packen
to coax [əu]	to get s.o. to do s.th. by kindness, patience, or flattery	schmeicheln, überreden
to be at stake	s. th. that might be won or lost according to the result of s. th.	auf dem Spiele stehen
I'd have to take to deeper layers of rouge [ru:ʒ]	I'd have to put on more make-up	ich müßte zu tieferen Rougeschichten Zuflucht nehmen
padding at the shoulders	material used to bolster up the shoulders of a suit for example	Wattierung, Polsterung
to wear a scent [sent]	to use a certain perfume	ein bestimmtes Parfum verwenden
tripping her fingers across his chest	moving her hand across his chest by lightly touching it with her fingers	indem sie ihre Finger über seinen Brustkasten tänzeln läßt

p. 82

bosom [ˈbuzəm]	breast	Busen
to be partial to s. b. [ˈpɑːʃəl]	having a liking for s. b.	für jmd eingenommen sein
freckles [ˈfreklz]	small light-brown spots on the human skin	Sommersprossen
aphrodisiac [ˌæfroˈdiziæk]	arousing or increasing sexual desire	Aphrodisiakum, Liebesmittel
trombone [trɔmˈbəun]	musical brass instrument with a sliding tube	Posaune
to reminisce [ˌremiˈnis]	to think or talk about past events and experiences	in Erinnerungen schwelgen, sich in Erinnerungen ergeben
to grab (hold of) s. th.	to take s. th. roughly, to snatch	hastig, gierig fassen/ergreifen
to keep the needle poised for attack	to hold the needle as if it were a weapon	die Nadel angriffsbereit hochhalten

p. 83

Victorian taste	prudish, conventional, narrow taste as developed under the reign of Queen Victoria (1837–1901)	prüder/unnatürlicher Geschmack; Viktorianischer G.
to strike s. th. off	to finish s. th. quickly and without care	etwas schnell hinhauen
to ponder s. th.	to think over, to consider	erwägen, überlegen, bedenken
post-coital depression [ˈpəust ˈkəuitəl]	a depression which is said to be sometimes felt after sexual intercourse	Niedergeschlagenheit nach dem Beischlaf

brothel manners ['brɔθəl]	manners as shown towards prostitutes or by prostitutes	Bordellmanieren
to rush s. b.	to cause s. o. to make haste	jmd (zu etwas) drängen
a lap (sport)	one course around a race track	eine Runde (beim Laufen)

p. 84

to sway the jury	to influence the jury in one's favour	die Geschworenen mitreißen, unter seinen Bann bekommen
testy, adv. testily	having an irritable disposition; touchy	gereizt, unwirsch
irrefutable [i'refjutəbl]	that cannot be proved false	unwiderlegbar
to be outraged at	to be annoyed at; to feel insulted	schockiert/empört sein über
an ordinance (against s. th.) ['ɔ:dinəns]	order given by an authority	amtliche Verordnung, Verfügung (gegen etw)
to solicit people [sə'lisit]	to make an enquiry; to ask people earnestly	(Leute) ansprechen; sich ernsthaft erkundigen
woolly-headed ['wuli'hedid]	stupid, silly	dumm, blödsinnig
sinus (med.) ['sainəs]	hollow in a bone communicating with the nose	Nasennebenhöhle
juror ['dʒuərə]	member of a jury	Geschworener

Caesarean [si:'zæriən]	the delivery of a child by section of the abdominal walls and the womb of the mother when ordinary delivery is apparently impossible	Kaiserschnitt
hermetically sealed	made air tight; impervious to air or liquids	hermetisch abgeschlossen
to bellow s. o. out	to shout at s. o. in order to intimidate him or give vent to one's anger	jmd anbrüllen, "zusammenschreien"

p. 85

caprice [kə'pri:s]	whim; sudden change of mind without any obvious cause	Laune, Launenhaftigkeit
to wiggle	(cause to) move with quick, short side-to-side movements	wackeln
non sequitur ['nɔn 'sekwitə]	a wrong conclusion; an inference that does not follow from the premises	Trugschluß; irrige Folgerung
to pat	to tap lightly and encouragingly	tätscheln, klatschen, klopfen
to skip s. th.	to omit s. th.; to avoid discussing a touchy subject	etwas beiseite lassen; etwas übergehen
scraps of facts	little bits of information	"Fetzen" von Tatsachen
chemistry formula ['kemistri]	H_2O is the chemistry formula for water	chemische Formel

impregnable [im'preg...]	proof against attack; s. th. that cannot be overcome or taken	uneinnehmbar, unüberwindlich

p. 86

wistful	having or showing a rather unsatisfied and often vague desire	sehnsüchtig, wehmütig
a suit for damages	a proceeding in a court of law in which a plaintiff demands the recovery of material losses	Klage auf Schadenersatz
to mash s. th. / s. o.	to squash; to mangle beyond recognition	(zu Brei) zerquetschen
brief case ['bri:f ...]	a leather portfolio for carrying briefs, manuscripts etc.	Aktentasche
attorney [ə'tə:ni]	person with legal authority to act for another in business or law	Rechtsanwalt
opposing attorney		Anwalt der Gegenseite
to probe (witnesses)	to investigate or examine thoroughly	sondieren, gründgründlich aushorchen
to soak up sympathetic stares	to attract compassionate looks	etwa: teilnahmsvolle Blicke auf sich ziehen
to incense [in'sens]	to make s. o. angry	erzürnen, in Rage bringen

hiccup ['hikʌp]	sudden stopping of the breath with a cough-like sound	Schluckauf
to blink	to wink rapidly; to look with half-closed eyes	blinzeln, zwinkern
to stand stunned	to stand unable to move or think	wie betäubt, wie gelähmt dastehen
to gulp	to gasp and choke from emotion	Tränen unterdrücken; vor Rührung schlucken
to jerk [dʒəːk]	to move quickly with spasmodic movements	ruckartig zucken; hochschnellen
frail	easily broken or destroyed; of delicate constitution	zerbrechlich, schwach, zart
to syncopate ['siŋkə,peit]	special beat in music	synkopieren
Calliope [kə'laiə,piː]	the muse of epic poetry	Kalliope (Muse der epischen Dichtung)
calliope	special sort of street organ	musik. Dampfpfeifenorgel

p. 87

apposite remarks ['æpəzit]	appropriate, fit remarks	angemessene, passende Bemerkungen
to be drowned out with laughter	become inaudible because of general laughter	im Gelächter untergehen; durch Gelächter unhörbar werden

timpano, pl.: -i ['timpənəu, pl.: -ai]	musical instrument	Kessel-, Orchesterpauke
to nudge s. b.'s ribs [nʌdʒ]	to touch or push gently, as with the elbow, in order to attract attention	(mit dem Ellenbogen) jmd in die Rippen stoßen
snickers	half suppressed or smothered laugh	Gekicher, Kichern
askew [ə'skju:]	= askance [ə'skæns]; awry	von der Seite; schief, schräg
spasm ['spæzəm]	convulsive, involuntary contraction of muscles	Krampf, Zuckung, Anfall
pertinent ['pə:tinənt]	being to the point; appropriate	zur Sache gehörig; angemessen
judicial [dʒu:'diʃəl]	pertaining to the law	gerichtlich; Gerichts ...
closure of the glottis ['kləuʒə, 'glɔtis]		in der Phonetik: Verschluß der Stimmritze
gibberish ['gibəriʃ; 'dʒib..]	incoherent or unintelligible talk	dummes Zeug, Quatsch, Kauderwelsch
a mole on the skin	a birthmark	Muttermal
an also-ran	one who participated in a competition, but did not have the slightest chance of winning	ein unbedeutender Mensch, einer der zu den "unter ferner liefen" gehört

p. 88

to snip off	to slice or cut off quickly in short pieces	wegschnippeln, abschneiden

birthmark	a mark or stain existing on the skin from birth	Muttermal
tucked behind her ear	hidden behind her ear	hinter ihrem Ohre versteckt
inconspicuously adv. [ˌinkən'spikjuəsli]	not attracting attention	unauffällig
to zone [zəun]	to divide into sections	in Zonen aufteilen
to zone to perfection	to lead gradually to perfection	Stück für Stück zur Vollkommenheit führen
with bristling hair ['brisliŋ]	with one's hair on end	mit gesträubtem Haar

p. 89

the goodies coll.	sweets, sweetmeat	Süßigkeiten, Bonbons
predictable [pri'diktəbl]	that can be predicted or foreseen	voraussagbar
rigid schedule ['ridʒid 'ʃedju:l]	a timed plan that cannot be altered	starrer Zeitplan, starres Schema
to be vexed at	to be angry, annoyed at	ärgerlich sein über
dizziness ['dizinis]	feeling as if everything were turning round	Schwindelanfall, Benommenheit
something live to string up [laiv]	some living creature that can be hanged	etwas Lebendiges zum Aufhängen
apprehension [ˌæpri'henʃən]	distrust or dread concerning the future	Befürchtung, Besorgnis

p. 90

noose [nuːs]	a loop furnished with a running knot	Schlinge
morgue [mɔːg]	a place where bodies of the dead are kept until identified	Leichenschauhaus
to tilt back	to lean backwards; to move backwards into a sloping position	zurückneigen, zurücklehnen
immaculate [iˈmækjulit]	pure; without spot or blemish	makellos, rein, unbefleckt
trap door	a door designed to close or fall at a slight disturbance so that the victim is captured	Falltür
the confines [ˈkɔnfainz]	= confinement	Begrenzung, Beengtheit
meek [iː]	gentle, humble; submissive	demütig, milde; unterwürfig
to convert s. b. to s. th.	to cause to change a person's beliefs	jmd bekehren
womb [wuːm]	organ in a female mammal in which offspring is carried before birth	Mutterleib, Gebärmutter
coarse talk	low and vulgar language, not refined	grobe, ungehobelte Redeweise
algebra equation [ˈældʒibrə iˈkweiʃən]	$a + a = 2a$ is an algebra equation	algebraische Gleichung

p. 91

still-life	the representation of fruit, flowers, lifeless animals or inanimate objects	Stilleben
whore [hɔ:]	prostitute	Hure
grease- stained [gri:-s]	stains on any material caused by fatty or oily substances	voller Fettflecken
kimono [ki'məunəu]	Japanese loose robe, imitated as an Occidental woman's négligée	Kimono; Damenmorgenrock
to fret over s. th.	to worry about; be dicontented	sich ärgern, sich kränken
whim [(h)wim]	sudden change of will without any apparent reason	Laune
to crack on s. th. coll.	to hit; to strike sharply	schlagen, hauen
inflamed	heated and swollen because of some infection	entzündet (Wunde)
genital tract ['dʒenitəl]		Fortpflanzungstrakt
to wheeze [(h)wi:z]	to breathe noisily	keuchen, schnaufen; pfeifend atmen
filing cabinet	case or drawers for keeping papers and documents	Aktenschrank

p. 92

seven- iron	apparently misspelled for: "sever- iron"	"Trennbeil"

debris ['deibri:, 'debri:]	ruins, rubbish	Trümmer, Schutt
dizzy	mentally confused, giddy	benommen, schwindelig

p. 93

to twitch with excitement	to be so excited that one cannot control the movements of one's limbs	vor Erregung/vor Aufregung zucken
obtrusive [əb'tru:-siv]	inclined to push oneself foreward; bothersome	aufdringlich, zudringlich
lever ['li:və]	a straight bar turning freely on a fixed point	Hebel
my head pounds	I have a dreadful headache	mein Kopf dröhnt/pocht
to nibble one's lip in fear	to bite one's lips from fear	sich vor Angst auf der Zunge herumbeißen
to panick [æ]	to become affected with sudden, unreasonable fear	in panische/sinnlose Angst geraten
hangover ['– –]	the aftereffects of alcoholic dissipation, such as headache etc.	"Katzenjammer", "Kater"

p. 94

hangover of the gallows		"Galgenkatzenjammer"
to strangle ['stræŋgl]	to kill by squeezing the throat	erdrosseln

to be bunched in twos	to be bound up in twos	zu zweien gebündelt sein
the cell is pushing in on you		die Zelle stürzt über einem zusammen

p. 95

JACK RICHARDSON

GALLOWS HUMOUR PART TWO

p. 97

executioner [ˌeksi'kju:ʃənə]	public official who executes prisoners	Henker, Scharfrichter
curler ['kə:lə]	devise for curling one's hair	Lockenwickler
dowdy ['daudi]	shabby, unfashionable; shabbily dressed	nachlässig gekleidet, schlampig
pepper-mill	container in which pepper corns are ground to powder	Pfeffermühle
conspicuous [kən'spikjuəs]	easily seen, remarkable	auffallend, auffällig
penal code ['pi:nəl]	a book in which laws are fixed	Strafgesetzbuch
headsman	here: executioner	Henker
hood [hud]	bag-like covering for the head and the neck	Kapuze
morbid ['mɔ:bid]	diseased	krankhaft, pathologisch

thumbscrew ['θʌmskru:]	device of torture in which the thumbs are squeezed	Daumenschraube
iron maiden ['aiən'meidən]	cage-like device in which the body of a prisoner can be pressed together	eiserne Jungfrau
unsanitary [ʌn'sænitəri]	not hygienic, unwholesome	unhygienisch, ungesund
dungeon ['dʌndʒən]	dark moist underground room, used as a prison	Verließ
oatmeal ['əutmi:l]	meal made from oats	Hafergrütze, Haferschleim

p. 98

crusty	having a crust, usually: crusted	mit einer Kruste überzogen, knusprig
exasperation [ig, zɑ:spə'reiʃən]	state of being exasperated, feeling irritation and anger	Erbitterung, Ärger
petulance ['petjuləns]	unreasonable impatience or irritibility	Verdrießlichkeit, Gereiztheit
finely edged	a knife or other instrument with a sharp edge	scharf geschliffen
to strangle ['stræŋgl]	to kill by squeezing the throat of s. b.	erdrosseln
to jeer at [dʒiə]	to mock, to laugh rudely at	verhöhnen, verspotten
to hiss	to show disapproval by making this sound	zischen
to scribble	to write hastily or carelessly	kritzeln
scribbles	meaningless and careless marks on paper	Gekritzel

bump	swelling on the body caused by a blow	Beule, Schwellung
crease [kri:s]	line made on cloth by folding and pressing	Bügelfalte
slit	long narrow cut, tear, or opening	Schlitz
to crackle	to make a series of small cracking sounds	knistern
perception [pəˈsepʃən]	process by which we become aware of things through the senses of sight and the power of the mind	sinnliche und geistige Wahrnehmung
to jut out	to stand out from, to be out of line	heraus-, hervorragen

p. 99

brass [ɑ:]	bright yellow metal made by mixing copper and zinc	Messing
optional [ˈɔpʃənəl]	which may be chosen or not according to one's wishes; not compulsory	wahlfrei, freiwillig, freigestellt
to plead [i:]	here: to offer as an explanation or as an excuse	inständig bitten, plädieren
to dangle [ˈdæŋgl]	to hang or swing loosely	baumeln, herabhängen
to relax [riˈlæks]	to cause or allow to become less tight, stiff or rigid	entspannen
digestion [diˈdʒestʃən, daiˈ...]	action of the stomach and the bowels by which food is transformed so that it can be used by the body	Verdauung

trout [au]	freshwater fish, valued as food and for the sport of catching it	Forelle
bait	food put on a hook in order to catch fish	Köder
to give in	to stop fighting or arguing; to surrender	nachgeben, aufgeben
to droop	to bend or hang downwards through tiredness or weakness	schlaff herabhängen, herabsinken (lassen)
scrambled eggs	cook eggs by beating them and then heating them up in a saucepan with butter	Rührei
stain	a coloured patch or dirty mark on s. th.	(Farb-, Schmutz-) Flecken
bone	here: material from which buttons are made	Horn, Fischbein

p. 100

to count on s. b.	to rely upon s. b.	mit jmd rechnen, auf jmd zählen
dejected [di'dʒektid]	discouraged, depressed	entmutigt, niedergeschlagen
to take out a joint bank account	a bank account from which several persons can withdraw money	ein gemeinsames Bankkonto einrichten
to be dotted with	strewn all over with	übersät, bestreut sein mit
erasure smudge [i'reiʒə smʌdʒ]	place where s. th. has been rubbed or scraped out	Schmierfleck, der von einer Radierung zurückbleibt

to be confined to	to be imprisoned, restrained in	eingesperrt sein in, beschränkt sein auf
to wobble	to move or sway unsteadily	schwanken, wakkeln, watscheln
a firm behind colloq	firm buttocks	ein draller Hintern
prosecutor ['prɔsi,kju:tə]	one who prosecutes in behalf of the state	Staatsanwalt, öffentlicher Ankläger
closet ['klɔzit]	small chamber; side room or recess for storing clothes	Kabinett, Geheimzimmer; Wandschrank

p. 101

to be tucked beneath the pillow	here: hidden away under the pillow	unter dem Kopfkissen versteckt sein
to squeeze [i:]	to press hard; to extract s. th. from by pressing	drücken, quetschen, pressen
string (of a banjo)	thin cord of an instrument	Saite (eines Instrumentes)
to snore [ɔ:]	to breathe noisily while sleeping	schnarchen
to pout [au]	to thrust out the lips in ill humour; to be sullen	schmollen; die Lippen aufwerfen
to ooze sympathy ['u:z 'simpəθi]	to make sympathy appear	Sympathie ausstrahlen
a stack (of plates, towels etc.)	a systematic pile or heap of s. th.	Stapel; geordneter Haufen
brief [i:]	short	kurz

p. 102

to donate [dəu′neit]	to bestow as a gift, to make a contribution	spenden, beisteuern
to put one's foot down colloq	to object, to protest, to be firm	energisch werden, ein Machtwort sprechen
a vigorous nod [′vigərəs]	a nod performed with vigour and energy	ein kräftiges Nicken
cut from the same timber	made from the same material; be the same	aus dem gleichen Holze geschnitzt
to turn nasty remarks about s. b.	to make nasty remarks about s. b.	über jmd boshafte Bemerkungen machen
to play s. b.'s game	to play the game according to s. b.'s own rules	sich nach denselben Spielregeln richten

p. 103

nostalgic(ally) [nɔs′tældʒik(əli)]	feeling or causing of homesickness; a longing for s. th. far away or long ago	an Heimweh leidend; wehmütig, sehnsüchtig
bloodshot eyes	eyes shot with blood; red and inflamed	blutunterlaufene, entzündete Augen
to pop	to make a short explosive sound, to burst open or explode with such a sound	platzen, knallen; platzen lassen
vessel	here: canal for transporting blood	Gefäß; Blutgefäß, Ader
to sample s. th. [ɑ:]	to test or examine by means of a sample	von etw Proben entnehmen

manual labourer ['mænjuəl 'leibərər]	one who works with his hands	Handarbeiter
in unison ['ju:nisən]	in accordance, in harmony	in Einklang
crib	here: baby cot	Krippe, Wiege; Babybett
to jeopardize ['dʒepədaiz]	to imperil, to endanger	gefährden

p. 104

to throw off the gloom	to brighten up, to cheer up	die düstere Stimmung abstreifen
to tumble out words	to utter words quickly, without reflection	Worte hervorsprudeln lassen
what size dress	what size of a dress	welche Kleidergröße
an engagement book	a calendar in which appointments and engagements are entered	Terminkalender
mischief ['mistʃif]	troublesome or damaging action or result; moral harm or injury	Unheil, Unfug; Posse
to catch up	here: to do all the work that has not yet been done	aufarbeiten, nachholen
dejected [di'dʒektid]	sad or gloomy; in low spirits	traurig; entmutigt
flat	smooth, level; dull, monotonous	flach; eintönig; lustlos

Cancer Fund meeting	a meeting arranged for considering means of raising money for the benefit of a society whose aim it is to fight cancer	Krebshilfetagung

p. 105

Parole Board [pə'rəul 'bɔːd]	committee in a prison that considers the release of prisoners from jail prior to the expiration of their term	Kommission für bedingte (= vorzeitige) Haftentlassung
moody [uː]	gloomy, bad tempered	launisch, übelgelaunt
to slink around	to go or move around stealthily	herumschleichen
to be sealed away	to be locked away for good	wegschließen; plombieren
immobile [i'məubail]	not able to move or be moved	unbeweglich, starr

p. 106

to muffle	to wrap or cover for warmth or protection	einhüllen, einwickeln
a muffled voice	speaking in a low voice	gedämpfte Stimme
ferocious [fi'rəuʃəs]	fiery, cruel	wild, grausam
to send a chill through s. b.	to make s. b. feel cold all over from shock or dismay	jmd erschauern lassen
to see s. th. to its best advantage	to consider only the bright aspects of s. th.	etw. im besten Lichte sehen

occurrence [əˈkʌrəns]	happening, event	Vorkommnis, Ereignis
to be stunned	here: to be shocked, confused	verblüfft, niedergeschmettert sein
plumber [ˈplʌmə]	workman who fits pipes, drains etc.	Klempner
grease [gri:s]	thick, semi-solid oily substance	Schmiere, Fett
predictable	that can be predicted	voraussagbar

p. 107

to joggle along	to move along as if by repeated jerks	dahinwackeln, vorwärtsruckeln
to joggle	to shake, to move by repeated jerks	rütteln, schütteln
to slither down [ˈsliðə]	to slide or slip down	hinabrutschen, hinabschlindern
drainpipe	pipe in a system of drains	Abflußrohr; hier: Regenrinne
to psychoanalyse [ˌsaikəuˈænəlaiz]	to analyse the events of a person's former life in order to find out the mental disorder of his present state of mind	eine Psychoanalyse machen
to keep to the rules of the game	to play fair and according to the rules	sich an die Spielregeln halten
to kick up one's heels	to revolt, to rebel	sich auflehnen
crack	line of division where s. th. is broken	Riß, Sprung

to stomach s. b. ['stʌmək]	to be able to stand s. b.	jmd ausstehen können; jmd ertragen können
during the foregoing [fɔː'gəuiŋ]	while the things decribed above were happening	während des Vorausgegangenen

p. 108

to speak in an official capacity [ə'fiʃəl kə'pæsiti]	to speak as a public officeholder and not as a private citizen	in offizieller Eigenschaft sprechen
subordinate [səb'ɔː:dinit]	junior in rank and position; less important	Untergebener; untergeordnet
platitude ['plæti,tjuː:d]	statement that is obviously true; a commonplace	Plattheit, Gemeinplatz; Plattitüde
trinket	ornament or jewel of small value	wertloses Schmuckstück
to contract a disease [di'ziː:z]	to get an infection	sich eine Krankheit zuziehen
leak [iː:]	hole caused by wear or injury	Leck, undichte Stelle
bad-breathed ['bæd,briː:ðd]	smelling bad from one's mouth	mit Mundgeruch
mutinous ['mjuː:tinəs]	guilty of mutiny; rebellious	meuternd, rebellisch
latitude ['læti,tjuː:d]	distance north or south of the equator	(geographische) Breite
longitude ['lɔndʒi,tjuː:d]	distance east or west from standard meridian	(geographische) Länge

curvaceous colloq [kə:'veiʃəs]	shapely in form; having voluptuous curves	'kurvenreich' (auf weiblichen Körper bezogen)
doldrums ['dɔldrəmz]	places on the earth without any wind movement	Kalmen, windstille Gebiete
in the doldrums	fig.: in low spirits	niedergeschlagen
being worn by rubbing	being worn thin	abgenutzt, abgescheuert
to poke about	to push, to feel about	herumstoßen, herumstochern
to flaunt [ɔ:]	to show off complacently	prunken, offen zeigen
flaunting well-laundered sails ['lɔ:ndəd]	showing clean-washed sails with pride	mit sauber gewaschenen Segeln prunken
to scrub	to clean by rubbing with brush, soap, and water	scheuern, schrubben
scurvy ['skə:vi]	disease caused by eating too much salt flesh and not enough fresh vegetables	Skorbut
to stick to the chart	to steer a vessel according to a fixed course on a sea map	den Kurs halten
to toss cargo overboard ['əuvəbɔ:d]	to throw load out of a ship into the water	Ladung über Bord werfen, Ballast abwerfen
sensible	reasonable	vernünftig
unmarketable [ʌn'ma:kətəbl]	things that nobody wants are unmarketable	unverkäuflich, nicht absetzbar
bauble ['bɔ:bl]	s. th. that nobody wants because it is of no value	Tand; Nippsache; Spielzeug

p. 109

dinghy ['dingi]	small open boat; inflatable rubber boat	Dinghi, Beiboot, Schlauchboot
to bob	to move up and down by jerks	(ruckweise) auf- und niederbewegen
to tighten the hatches	to fasten the openings of a ship	die Luken dichtmachen
to secure the rigging [si'kjuə]	to fasten parts of a ship such as masts, sails etc.	die Takelage sichern
mermaid ['mə:meid]	woman with a fish's tail instead of legs	Meerjungfrau
he edged his way to the door	he carefully moved towards the door	er schob sich (vorsichtig) zur Tür
lifeboat	boat carried on a ship for use in case the ship gets into the danger of sinking	Rettungsboot
to rescue ['reskju:]	to save; to set free	retten
to sprout	to begin to grow	sprießen
flimsy	light and thin	zerbrechlich, dünn
band-aid	first aid band	Notverband

p. 110

to hint at s. th.	to make a slight or indirect suggestion	auf etw hinweisen, etw andeuten
brass [ɑ:]	bright and yellow metal, made by mixing copper and zinc	Messing

it never ocurred to me	I never thought of it	es kam mir nie in den Sinn
to envy ['envi]	feel disappointment at another's good luck	beneiden
travel folders	papers with advertisements of a travel agency	Reiseprospekte; Faltprospekte

p. 111

tweed [i:]	thick, soft, woolen cloth	Tweedstoff
to break out in a rash	to get tiny red spots on the skin	einen Hautausschlag bekommen
to shimmer	to shine with a waving soft of faint light	warm leuchten, glänzen
to sway	to move unsteadily from one side to the other	schwanken
a sleight-of-hand trick ['slaitəv'hænd]	expertness in using one's hands in performing tricks	Taschenspielertrick
to retrieve s. th.	to regain s. th.; here: to take s. th. back	wiedererlangen, zurücknehmen
mirage [mi'rɑ:ʒ; 'mi..]	effect produced by hot air	Luftspiegelung, Fata Morgana
to escort [is'kɔ:t]	to accompany in order to protect or in token of homage	geleiten, eskortieren
reprimand ['repri,mɑ:nd]	official rebuke	Verweis, Rüge, Maßregelung

p. 112

my superiors [sju:'piəriəz]	persons of higher rank than I	meine Vorgesetzten

to open one's pores [pɔ:z]	so as to sweat out anything unhealthy	die Poren öffnen
coffee grounds	particles of coffee that sink to the bottom	Kaffeesatz, -grund
to rinse	to wash with clean water	ausspülen, abspülen
passable ['pɑ:səbl]	moderate, not too good, fairly good	passabel, einigermaßen
to humour s. o.	to gratify s. o.'s whims, give in to s. o.	jmd bei Laune halten; jmd Willen tun
to do free-lance work	to work for anyone without being dependent on him	freiberuflich tätig sein
to have an eye peeled for ..	to keep a watch on	ein wachsames Auge für ... haben
to prune [u:]	to cut away branches of trees or bushes in order to control their growth	(Bäume, Büsche) stutzen, beschneiden
weeds [i:]	small plants in a garden that are not wanted	Unkraut
to teem with [i:]	to have in very great numbers, to be brimful with	wimmeln vor
centipede ['senti,pi:d]	small insect-like creature with a long thin body, numerous joints, and a pair of feet at each joint	Tausendfüßler
middle-income housing development	an area in which arable land is being transformed into a place in which houses for people of middle income will be built	Baulanderschließung für Häuser von Leuten mit mittleren Einkommen

agleam [ə'gli:m]	shining softly; with soft light in one's eyes	glänzend, strahlend

p. 113

to stalk s. th. [ɔ:]	to move cautiously towards wild animals in order to get near them	sich anschleichen an
insecticide [in'sekti,said]	poison used to kill insects	Insektenbekämpfungsmittel Insektizid
to stuff oneself with just the exact calorie count ['kæləri]	to eat exactly the amount of food that is sufficient for one's health	sich mit genau der richtigen Kalorienzahl vollstopfen
to leave the proper tip	tips are obligatory in the USA; they amount from 10 to 15 %; the money is simply left on the table	das genau erforderliche Trinkgeld zurücklassen
to peek	to look quickly	flüchtig gucken, blicken
an off-colour joke	a joke that is neither witty nor good	ein etwas farbloser Witz
to pat s. b.	to tap s. b. gently	tätscheln, klopfen
gleam	beam or ray of soft light	schwacher Schein, schwacher Lichtstrahl
to do s. b. in sl	to kill s. b.	jmd 'kaltmachen'
funeral arrangements ['fju:nərəl]	preparations for burying s. b.	Vorbereitungen zur Bestattung
epitaph ['epitɑ:f]	words on a tombstone, describing the dead person	Grabinschrift, Epitaph

p. 114

to confide in s. b.	to have faith in s. b.	jmd vertrauen
gesture ['dʒestʃə]	movement of the hand or head to indicate an idea or feeling	Geste, Gebärde
to speak up	to utter one's opinion without hesitation or fear	laut und deutlich sprechen, kein Blatt vor den Mund nehmen
to pick up and leave	to take one's things and go away	seine Sachen packen und gehen
a dentist appointment	a date fixed for the meeting with the dentist	Termin beim Zahnarzt
molar ['məulə]	one of the teeth used for grinding food	Mahl-, Backenzahn
to be partial ['pɑːʃəl]	to take sides for, to be interested in	eingenommen sein für; etw übrighaben für
chocolate mousse ['tʃɔklit'muːs]	dish of chocolate cream beaten and frozen	Schokoladencreme
weekend whirl [wəːl]	rapid succession of activities during the weekend	Wochenendtrubel, Wochenendwirbel
to put on schedule ['ʃedjuːl, Am: 'skedʒl]	to enter in a list of arrangements	planen, vorsehen

p. 115

to start blooming	to begin to bear flowers; here: (ironically) to become young again	aufblühen, in die zweite Jugend kommen

things pop up	things come quickly and unexpectedly	Dinge tauchen plötzlich auf
to detain s. b. [di'tein]	to keep s. b. waiting, to keep s. b. back	jmd zurückhalten, aufhalten
to sweep the old laws under the rug	to abolish the old laws as if they were rubbish	die alten Gesetze 'unter den Teppich fegen'
obstacle ['ɔbstikl]	s. th. in the way that stops progress or makes it difficult	Hindernis
to chop down	to cut down by blows with an axe or other edged tool	umhacken, niederhauen
to paw over s. b. [pɔ:]	to touch with the hands awkwardly or rudely	jmd 'befummeln'
snug	warm and comfortable; sheltered	warm, behaglich; geborgen
underground plumbing ['plʌmiŋ]	the pipes, watertanks etc in a building	verdeckte Rohrleitungen
to snip apart	cut asunder, cut in two	auseinanderschnippeln
three letter word	referring to the conjunction 'and' in man 'and' wife	Wort aus drei Buchstaben

p.116

law of gravity ['græviti]	'all objects are drawn towards the centre of the earth'	Gravitationsgesetz
to yank colloq	to give a sudden sharp pull; tug	(mit einem Ruck) ziehen, reißen
to tug at s. th.	to pull at s. th.	an etw ziehen
damp	not thoroughly dry; moist	feucht

dampness	moisture on the surface or existing throughout	Feuchtigkeit, Feuchtigkeitsgehalt
to taunt [ɔ:]	to attack s. b. by making fun of him	sticheln, reizen
taunt	remark intended to hurt s. b.	Stichelei, Spöttelei
stubborn ['stʌbən]	difficult to deal with; obstinate	dickköpfig, eigensinnig
rubber girdle ['gə:dl]	rubber corset or belt fastened round the waist to keep clothes in position	Gummikorsett; Hüfthalter aus Gummi
to yell at s. b.	to shout or cry at s. b.	jmd anschreien
hinge [hindʒ]	joint on which a lid, door, or gate swings	(Tür)angel, Scharnier
to pound on	to strike heavily and repeatedly at/on s. th.	kräftig draufschlagen, drauftrommeln
athlete's foot ['æθli:ts 'fut]	ringworm of the foot, caused by a parasitic fungus	Fußpilz, Dermatophylose
diarrhoea [ˌdaiə'ri:ə]	too frequent emptying of the bowels	Durchfall
joint	place or point where bones are joined	Gelenk
paunchy [ɔ:]	getting wide round the waist	dick(bäuchig)

p. 117

an obedient attitude [ə'bi:diənt]	showing respect and obedience	unterwürfige Haltung
menacing ['menəsiŋ]	threatening	drohend

incredulous [in'kredjuləs]	unbelieving, showing disbelief	ungläubig
to do s. b. in colloq	to kill s. b.	jmd 'kaltmachen', umbringen
to fill out a blank in triplicate ['triplikit]	to fill out three copies of a blank	ein Formular in dreifacher Ausfertigung anfertigen
to snap s. b.'s neck	here: to break s. b.'s neck	jmd den Hals brechen
ominous ['ɔminəs]	of bad omen, threatening	unheilverkündend, unheimlich
don't be an ass sour ['sauə]	don't be silly bad-tempered	sei nicht albern übellaunig, 'sauer'

p. 118

with her neck thrust out	she suddenly sticks out her head	sie streckt (plötzlich) ihren Hals vor
windpipe	passage for air from the throat to the lungs	Luftröhre
incentive [in'sentiv]	that which incites, rouses or encourages	Anreiz, Antrieb
ivy plants ['aivi]	climbing, clinging, evergreen plants	Efeuranken
to focus one's eyes on	to concentrate one's eyes on	etw scharf ins Auge fassen
this is the closest we have come to sex in years	this somewhat sadistic experience was the only sexual relationship we have had for years	seit Jahren sind wir uns sexuell nicht so nahe gekommen

to grow stooped [stu:pt]	one's back being bent forward by age	krumm, gebeugt werden
sloppy	unsystematic, not done with care	schlampig, nachlässig
you should be gagging colloq	you should hold your tongue now	du solltest jetzt schweigen

p. 119

to mop one's brow	to wipe away sweat from one's forehead	Schweiß von der Stirn wischen
docile ['dəusail]	easily trained or controlled	fügsam, gefügig
nose drops, cough syrup ['kɔ:f 'sirəp]	medicine against a cold	Nasentropfen, Hustensaft
certificate of merit [sə:'tifikit]	written statement of merit	Führungszeugnis; Bescheinigung über gute Führung
pension bonus ['penʃən 'bəunəs]	payment to what is usually paid as pension	Pensionszulage
a retirement dinner [ri'taiəmənt]	the dinner of dismissal or farewell	Abschiedsessen
insurance policy [in'ʃuərəns'pɔlisi]	written statement of the terms of a contract of insurance	Versicherungspolice, Versicherungsschein

p. 120

to flip	to throw by the snap of the finger	schnippen, 'flipsen'

Murray Schisgal

THE TYPISTS

p. 123

British Drama League [li:g]	an association of British dramatists, playwrights, actors	
to tape for television	to record the sound and pictures of a play on the magnetic tape of a video--recorder	eine Bandaufnahme fürs Fernsehen machen
Edinburgh Festival ['edinbərə]	series of perfomances of music, ballet, drama given once a year in Edinburgh	Edinburger Festspiele
to take an option on ['ɔpʃən]	to obtain the right or power of choosing or rejecting s. th.	das Vorkaufsrecht (= Optionsrecht) für etwas erwerben
to write a scenario [si'nɑ:riəu]	to write the version of a play or novel in a film-production with details of the scenes	ein Drehbuch schreiben
movie company	a company in which several movies are united for the sake of business	Filmgesellschaft
unique [ju'ni:k]	being the only one of its sort	einzig(artig)

shibboleth ['ʃibə,leθ]	old-fashioned and now generally abandoned test of social correctness	Erkennungs-Losungswort
commercial feasibility [kə'mə:ʃəl fizi'biliti]	the performance of a play is commercially feasible if you make money by it	wirtschaftliche Durchführbarkeit
to dismay [dis'mei]	to frighten, to fill with the feeling of fear and discouragement	in Schrecken versetzen, entsetzen

p. 125

at twenty-odd years of age	the time of life between twenty and thirty	in den Zwanzigern (beim Lebensalter)
leaf, pl. leaves	hinged or loose part of an extending table which is used to make the table larger	Tischklappe; Einlegebrett beim Ausziehtisch
with leaves extended		mit ausgezogenen Klappen
a stack of cards	a pile or heap of cards	ein Stapel, ein Packen Karten
bulky [ʌ]	taking up much space, clumsy to move or carry	umfangreich, massig; sperrig
telephone directory ['telifəun di'rektəri]	list of names and addresses in ABC order of telephone owners	Telefonverzeichnis
rear [riə]	back part; in or at the back part	Hintergrund; hinterer ...
imperceptibility [impə,septi'biliti]	that cannot be perceived; very slight or gradual	Unmerklichkeit

imperceptible adj		unmerklich
subtle [sʌtl]	difficult to perceive or describe because fine and delicate	fein, hintergründig, subtil, raffiniert
cabinet ['kæbinit]	piece of furniture with drawers or shelves for storing or displaying things	(Büro-, Kartei-, Labor-) Schrank

p. 126

prompt person	person acting without delay	eine unverzüglich handelnde Person, eine prompte P.
supervisor ['sju:pə,vaizə]	person who watches and directs work and workers or an organisation	Aufseher

p. 127

to fall apart	to fall to pieces	auseinanderfallen
a substitute for ['sʌbsti,tju:t]	person or thing taking the place of or acting for another	Ersatz für
a promotion campaign [prə'məuʃən, kæm'pein]	advertising campaign in order to start off some new article	Werbeaktion; Werbefeldzug
mean [i:]	lacking generosity, selfish, nasty	niederträchtig, gemein
rusty	here: out of practice	'eingerostet', aus der Übung
to raise the roof colloq	to create an uproar, to make a great noise	jmd die 'Hölle heiß machen'

posture ['pɔstʃə]	position of the body, attitude	Körperhaltung
key	here: operating part of a typewriter	Tastatur
buzzer	electric hooter as used in an office to call s. b.	Summer, elektrische Klingel
to cover up (a mistake)	to hide s. th. in order to prevent its detection	verdecken, vertuschen, verbergen
hip	part on either side where the bone of the leg is joined to the trunk	Hüfte
he's got some goddam nerve ['gɔdæm]	he is really impudent	der hat vielleicht 'nen Nerv; der spinnt wohl'
to bawl s. b. out for s. th. [bɔ:-l] Am colloq	to scold s. b. severely	jmd anschnauzen, anbrüllen wegen etw
to associate with [ə'səuʃieit]	to be often in the company of	sich anschließen, sich zugesellen

p. 129

out of a sense of loyalty ['lɔiəlti]	out of a feeling of devotion or faithfulness	aus einem Gefühl der Loyalität (= Treue)
a sex maniac ['meiniæk]	someone obsessed by sex	Triebverbrecher, Sexbesessener
it stands to reason	it is quite obvious	es ist doch klar

deliberate [di'libərət]	done on purpose, intentional	absichtlich, überlegt
to quit one's job	to give up one's job, resign from a position	eine Arbeitsstelle aufgeben, kündigen
at my convenience [kən'vi:niəns]	how and when it best suits me	wenn es **mir** paßt
now you're talking	now you are right	so ist's recht; jetzt liegst du richtig
riot ['raiət]	violent burst of lawlessness; here: an uproariously amusing person	Aufruhr; hier: tolle Person; 'zum Schreien komisch'
caricature ['kærikə'tju:ə]	picture of a person making use of ridiculous exaggeration or distortion	Karikatur, Spottbild, Zerrbild
anomyous [ə'nɔniməs]	without a name, not signed	anonym; ohne Namensangabe
to be as blind as a bat	to be completely blind	blind wie eine Fledermaus
he used to have loose hands	he used to molest girls sexually, especially those dependent on him	'er konnte seine Hände nicht bei sich behalten'
(insurance) policy ['pɔlisi]	written statement of the terms of a contract of insurance	Versicherungspolice, Versicherungsschein
they were at each other's throats	they were fighting each other	sie sprangen einander an die Kehle
a run-down house	a shabby and dilapidated house	ein heruntergekommenes Haus

p.131

to throw up	here: to vomit	sich erbrechen, sich übergeben
kerbstone ['kə:b,stəun]	stone forming the edge of a raised pavement	Rinnstein
the left-overs	things that are not wanted any more	das Übriggebliebene, die Reste
onyx stones ['ɔniks]	quartz in layers of different colours; used for ornaments	Onyx Steine (Halbedelsteine)

p. 132

incommensurate [,inkə'menʃərət]	not comparable in respect of size; not worthy to be measured; having no common measure	unmeßbar mit; unvergleichlich; unmäßig, unbändig
mad Am	B. E.: cross, angry	ärgerlich, böse
to erase [i'reiz]	to rub or scrape out, pencil marks for instance	ausradieren

p. 133

to plug away colloq	to work hard at	hart arbeiten, schuften
to hold down a job	to keep a job (by showing that one is capable)	eine Stelle behaupten
glum	gloomy, sad	traurig, düster
what am I knocking myself out for?	why do I work so hard?	warum schufte ich mich so ab?
ditch-digger	a man who digs ditches	Grabenbauer, -zieher

to be on the ball	to be alert and competent	'am Ball sein'
an outfit this big	an enterprise of this size	ein Unternehmen dieser Größe
kid Am colloq	child; young person	Kind, Knirps; junger Mensch

p. 134

rascal [ɑ:]	dishonest person, rogue	Schuft, Schurke
chances for advancement	chances for promotion, for improvement	Aufstiegschancen; Chancen zur Beförderung
on the sales staff	a member of those employees that are responsible for the selling of goods	in der Verkaufsabteilung, im Verkauf
raise	here: a pay raise	Gehaltsaufbesserung

p. 135

lapel [lə'pel]	part of the front of a coat, attached to the collar	Rockaufschlag, Revers
her emotions soaring	she is getting more and more excited	ihre Gefühle werden immer stürmischer
dumb [dʌm]	refraining from speaking, mute, silent	stumm, sprachlos

p. 136

mayonnaise ['meiə,neiz]	a mixture of oil, vinegar, eggs and condiments	Mayonnaise

layer cake ['leiə]	a cake with horizontal divisions, seperated by cream, jam etc	Schichtkuchen, Torte
almond ['ɑ:mənd]	kernel of a fruit with pale brown colour	Mandel
veal parmesan ['vi:l ˌpɑ:mi'zæn]	an Italian speciality	Kalbfleisch mit Parmesankäse
chicken cacciatore ['kattʃa'tɔ:rə]	an Italian speciality	Hühnchen nach Jägerart

p. 137

you just keep that up ..	if you go on like that you will face unpleasant consequences	mach nur weiter so ...
I loathe you [ləuð]	I can't stand you, I hate you	ich verabscheue dich

p. 138

ravenous ['rævənəs]	violently hungry	heißhungrig, gefräßig
lethargic(ally) [le'θɑ:dʒik(əli)]	apathetic, dull, sleepy	lethargisch, träge, stumpf

p. 139

an 85 average ['ævəridʒ]	the normal intelligence quotient (IQ) being 100, 85 is quite a lot below average	weit unter Durchschnitt begabt
not by any stretch of the imagination	not even if one were willing to believe, could one believe	.. auch wenn man die Phantasie noch so strapaziert

remainder	rest, left-over	Rest, Überbleibsel
she swings the carriage across	she begins a new line on the typewriter	sie bringt die Schreibmaschine schwungvoll wieder in Ausgangsstellung
carriage of a typewriter	that part which carries the sheets of paper	Schlitten einer Schreibmaschine
to lilt	to sing or speak in light rhythmic manner	fröhlich, beschwingt singen oder sprechen
lilting intonation	rhythmic intonation	rhythmische Intonation
gumdrop ['gʌmdrɔp]	a molded sweetmeat, mostly soft inside	'Gummibärchen'
bag of candy	bag in which sweetmeats are kept	Beutel mit Süßigkeiten
to be on relief	to be given help in the form of food, clothes, money because one is in distress	Wohlfahrtsempfänger sein

p. 141

to wag (one's finger)	to move one's finger lightly from side to side in order to show disapproval	mit dem Finger drohen
smoke screen	a dense cloud of smoke emitted to hide an attack	Vernebelung; Rauchschutzschleier

p. 142

to pamper s. o.	to treat s. o. too indulgently, spoil s. b.	verhätscheln, verwöhnen

p. 143

for your information	expression used here to emphasize the indignation of the remark that follows	zu Ihrer Information; damit Sie es wissen!
I wouldn't trade her for a dozen like you	I wouldn't exchange her for anything	ich würde sie nicht für ein Dutzend Ihresgleichen eintauschen
to rave about s. th.	to speak wildly or incoherently about s. th.	über etw phantasieren, faseln; toben, rasen
jealous ['dʒeləs]	demanding exclusive worship and love; suspicious, watchful	eifersüchtig

p. 144

to crumple [ʌ]	to press or crush into folds and creases	zerknittern, zerknüllen
to punch s. b. in the nose	to strike s. b.'s nose hard with the fist	jmd mit der Faust ins Gesicht schlagen

p. 145

to lick s. b.'s boots	to show excessive praise or respect to s. o. in order to win his favour	vor jmd kriechen, bei jmd Speichel lecken

p. 146

to have the guts to colloq	to have the courage and determination to	den 'Mumm' haben zu .., den Mut haben zu ...
son-of-a-bitch Am	vulgar swear word; son of a prostitute	'Hurensohn', 'Scheißkerl'
bitch	female of a dog, and a human female who deliberately uses her sexual attraction to get men round her	Hündin; Nutte; Luder
.. that amounted to a bag of beans	that was of any importance	.. was irgend was wert war

p. 147

to slump down	to fall heavily down	in sich zusammensacken, niederplumpsen

p. 148

pretension [pri'tenʃən]	statement of a claim; claiming great merit or importance (without justification)	Anspruch, Anmaßung, Dünkel
entertainer ['entə ...]	s. b. who amuses others	Unterhalter, Conferencier

p. 149

inadvertently [,inəd'və:tntli]	(of actions) not done on purpose	unabsichtlich, versehentlich

knickers ['nikəz]	woman's or girl's undergarment reaching from the waist to the thighs	Damenschlüpfer

p. 150

haunch [ɔ:]	part of the body round the hips	Lende; pl. Gesäß

ARTHUR MILLER

INCIDENT AT VICHY

p. 155

detention	from 'to detain': keep waiting, keep back	Inhaftierung, Festnahme, Haft
a place of detention	a place where arrested people are kept waiting for being interrogated	ein Platz für Festgenommene
turning	place where a road or a corridor branches off or turns	Gabelung, Abzweigung
grimey [ai]	covered with dirt	schmutzig, rußig, beschmiert
window pane	a sheet of glass in the division of a window	Fensterscheibe
it suggests a warehouse	it makes one think that it is a warehouse	es läßt ein Lagerhaus vermuten
armoury ['ɑ:məri]	place where arms are kept	Waffenlager, -kammer

frieze ['fri:z]	ornamental band or strip along a wall with a special design	Fries; Zierstreifen (in der Architektur)
mutual ['mju:tjuəl]	(of feelings): shared, exchanged equally	gegenseitig
unobtrusive [,ʌnəb'tru:siv]	not too obvious, not easily noticeable	unaufdringlich, unauffällig
calling card	visiting card	Visitenkarte
unkempt	untidy; with one's hair dishevelled	unordentlich, ungepflegt; zerzaust
a sip of coffee	a small mouthful of coffee	ein Schlückchen Kaffee

p. 156

austerity [ɔ:'steriti]	quality of behaving severely moral and strict	Strenge, Einfachheit, Nüchternheit
muscular austerity	with the movements of the limbs reduced to what is absolutely necessary	etwa: sparsame Bewegungen
to shrug	to lift the shoulders slightly so as to show doubt, ignorance, or resignation	mit den Achseln zucken
an international police paint	the colour of the paint that is used by all policeforces makes those places look repellent	internationale Polizeifarbe
clam [æ]	a large shell-fish, with a shell in two halves, used for food	(eßbare) Muschel
alongside prep. to relax Am	close to, parallel with here: to become free from nervous tension	neben, längsseitig entspannen

p. 157

he shifts in his seat	he changes repeatedly his position	er bewegt sich auf dem Platz
with subdued anxiety [æŋ'zaiəti]	with the anxiety under control	mit unterdrückter Angst
a routine identity check [ru'ti:n ai'dentiti]	routine examination of identity cards and passports	Routineüberprüfung der Personalien
inevitable [in'evitəbl]	that cannot be avoided	unvermeidlich
flavour ['fleivə]	sensation of taste and smell	Geschmack(s-sinn); Aroma, Duft
profile ['prəufail]	side view of the head	Profil, Seitenansicht

p. 158

a dumb beast [dʌm]	an animal that cannot speak	ein stummes Geschöpf
a visa ['vizə] (no pl.)	stamp or signature on an passport to show that it has been examined and approved	Visum, Sichtververmerk
brass [ɑ:]	a bright yellow metal obtained by mixing copper and zinc	Messing
fourth-rate	of very low quality	viertklassig, minderwertig
crockery ['krɔkəri]	pots, plates, and other utensils made of clay	irdenes Geschirr; Steingut, Töpferware

p. 159

peak [i:]	the highest top of a mountain; the highest point	(Berg)spitze, Höhepunkt
you're talking utter confusion	what you say is completely incomprehensible	Sie reden völlig wirres Zeug
Goddammit [gɔ'dæmit]	swearword, esp. in the USA	Gottverdammt
to stroll (down)	to walk in a leisurely, unhurried way	(hinab)schlendern
sotto voce ['sɔtəu'vəutʃi:]	in a low voice; aside	halblaut; leise; beiseite
to break an appointment	not to go to a meeting although one has fixed the time and the place for it	eine Verabredung nicht einhalten
frayed (out)	worn by constant use	abgenutzt, durchgescheuert
felt hat	a hat pressed from soft material	Filzhut
posture ['pɔstʃə]	attitude of the body	(körperliche) Haltung
counterfeit papers ['kauntəfit]	falsified, imitated papers	gefälschte Papiere

p. 160

anomosity [ˌæni'mɔsiti]	strong dislike, active enmity	Animosität, Groll; Feindseligkeit
manpower shortage	not having enough men	Mangel an Arbeitskräften

to economize on personnel [iˈkɔnəmaiz; pəːsəˈnel]	to reduce the number of persons	Personal einsparen
I'm scared to death	I'm frightened out of my wits	ich habe wahnsinnige Angst
gypsy [ˈdʒipsi]	also spelled: gipsy; member of a wandering Asiatic tribe, living in many parts of Europe	Zigeuner
to bother s. b. [ˈbɔðə]	to worry s. b.: to cause s. b. trouble	belästigen
to fix s. th. Am	to repair s. th.	etw. flicken, in Ornung bringen
gloom	here: feeling of sadness and hopelessness	Schwermut; Düsterkeit
pressed pants	ironed trousers	gebügelte Hosen

p. 161

to whine [ai]	to utter complaing sounds like a dog	winseln
shrubbery [ʌ]	a cluster of bushes or shrubs	Strauchwerk, Gebüsch
they're on everybody's back	they are a burden for everybody	sie sitzen jedermann im Nacken
wan [ɔ]	pale, not bright, looking ill	blaß, kränklich
there is something ill about him	he seems to suffer from some illness	er sieht irgendwie krank aus

a limp	an uneven walk because one of the legs is shorter or crippled	Humpeln, Hinken

p. 162

bum [ʌ]	part of the body on which ohne sits; Am sl: habitual beggar or loafer	Hintern; Stromer, Strolch
S.S. ['es'es]	abbr. for Schutzstaffel: special body guard of Hitler, later on nazi military units	(Waffen-)SS
S.S. bums	those S.S. beggars	die SS-Strolche
to affect to do s. th. [ə'fekt]	to pretend to do s. th.	vortäuschen, zur Schau tragen
deferential [,defə'renʃəl]	showing respect	ehrerbietig, rücksichtsvoll
to be in charge of	to be responsible for	die Verantwortung tragen für; betraut sein mit
procedure [prə'si:dʒə]	regular order of doing legal things	juristisches Verfahren; Verfahrensweise
the door has been closed on his line	the door before which he is queuing has been shut	die Tür, vor der er in einer Schlange wartet, ist geschlossen worden
to glare at [ɛə]	to stare angrily or fiercely at	wild anstarren
eager for some clue [u:]	wanting to get some explanation	gespannt auf einen Hinweis
an identity check [ai'dentiti]	an examination of passports	Personalkontrolle

p. 163

sackcloth ['sækklɔθ]	strong material of coarse flax or hemp	Sackleinen
to release one's hold on [ri'li:s]	to set s. b. free; to allow s. b. to go	jmd loslassen, freilassen
combat officer ['kɔmbæt]	officer with the fighting army	Frontoffizier
the Occupation	the German occupation of France during the Second World War	die (deutsche) Besatzungszeit (1940–1943)
to revoke a law	to cancel or withdraw a law	ein Gesetz aufheben, widerrufen
to cruise around [kru:z]	of ships: to sail around; here: to walk about looking for wanted persons	'herumkreuzen'
rumour ['ru:mə]	general talk, gossip, hearsay	Gerücht

p. 164

croissant [krwasã] French	a small crescent-shaped roll	Hörnchen (Gebäck)
in a fever of calculation ['fi:və]	in an excited, nervous state because of his fears and misgivings	in fieberhaften Vermutungen
to grow cautious ['kɔ:ʃəs]	to become careful so as not to make a mistake	vorsichtig werden

p. 165

the bridge of the nose	upper bony part of the nose	Nasenrücken

the tip of the nose	the extreme part of the nose	Nasenspitze
detour ['di:tuə]	a roundabout way used when the main road is blocked	Umweg, Umleitung
forced labour	hard work that is forced upon s. o. against his will	Zwangsarbeit
to quote s. b.	to repeat s. b.'s words	zitieren, anführen
switchman ['switʃmən]	man in charge of railway switches or points by which a train can move from one track to another	Weichensteller
a round-up ['– –]	driving or bringing together of animals or men	Zusammentreiben, Zusammentrommeln
to double the rations ['ræʃənz]	to double the amount of food to which one is entitled	die Rationen verdoppeln

p. 166

to apply the Racial Laws ['reiʃəl 'lɔ:z]	in the Third Reich Jews were persecuted because their race was held to be inferior	die Rassengesetze anwenden
inscrutable [in'skru:təbl]	that cannot be understood or known, mysterious	unergründlich
to have a prejudice against s. o. ['predʒədis]	to dislike s. o. before one has adequately come to know him	ein Vorurteil gegen jmd haben

p. 168

to grab s. b.	to seize s. o. roughly or unexpectedly	packen, fassen; 'schnappen'

bolt [əu]	mostly a metal fastening for a door or window	Riegel
screwdriver ['skru:,draivə]	an instrument for turning screws	Schraubenzieher
chisel ['tʃizəl]	a steel tool for shaping wood, stone, or metal	Meißel
bricklaying	building with bricks; work done by a mason	Maurerarbeit
resettlement	helping people to find homes in a new country	Wiederbesiedlung, Umsiedlung

p. 168

to keep a sense of proportion	to retain a matter-of-fact view of things	einen Sinn für die richtigen Größenordnungen haben
Fascist ['fæʃist]	an aggressive nationalist and anticommunist	Faschist
psychoanalytic [,saikəuænə'litik]	examining the hidden motives of the soul	psychoanalytisch
Viennese [vie'ni:z]	belonging to or coming from Vienna	wienerisch; Wiener
to commit a gaffe [gæf]	to make an indiscreet remark or a blunder	einen Fauxpas begehen, eine Dummheit machen

p. 169

resentment toward [ri'zentmənt]	ill feeling against s. o., because one feels insulted or offended	Ressentiment, Groll gegen

to draw s. b. out	to get information out of s. b. by hiding the fact from him that he is questioned	jmd aushorchen, jmd 'ausnehmen'
nobleman	a representative of the aristocracy	Adliger
reactionary régime [ri'ækʃənəri rei'ʒi:m]	a government or administration that opposes progress or reform	reaktionäres Regime
to presume [pri'zju:m]	to suppose; to take for granted	vermuten, annehmen
to pry into s. b's affairs	to inquire too curiously into s. b.'s business	in jmd Angelegenheiten herumschnüffeln

p. 170

that's not the issue ['isju:; Am 'iʃu:]	that is not the point	darauf kommt es nicht an; das ist nicht das Problem
standing	established position; reputation	Rang, Stellung
Nazism ['nɑ:tsizm]	the ideology of the German National Socialist Party founded by Hitler	Nationalsozialismus
an outburst of vulgarity [vʌl'gæriti]	an eruption or explosion of the lowest instincts	ein Ausbruch des Vulgären
refinement [ri'fainmənt]	good taste for what is beautiful and decent	gebildetes Wesen, feiner Geschmack
a grocery clerk [klɑ:k]	the assistent in a grocery shop	Lebensmittelverkäufer

to be sensitive to	to feel very easily	empfindlich sein gegenüber
nuance ['njuəns; Am nu'æns]	delicate difference in shade of meaning, opinion, colour	Nuance; feiner Unterschied

p. 171

to be deeply at a loss	to be very perplexed	in großer Verlegenheit sein
in an amateur way ['æmətə]	for the love of a thing, not for money; not as an expert or a professional	als Amateur, als Liebhaber; als Dilettant

p. 172

phoney ['fəuni]	sham, not genuine	unecht, gefälscht, verlogen

p. 173

to pitch forward	to fall heavily forward	hinstürzen, hinschlagen
gentile ['dʒentail]	person that does not belong to the Jewish race	Nichtjude
to demoralize [di'mɔrəlaiz]	to weaken the courage and confidence	demoralisieren, entmutigen

p. 174

sadistic [sə'distik]	sadism ['seidizm] is a kind of sexual perversion; a sadist tries to get pleasure out of the cruelty to other people	sadistisch

p. 175

suspect ['sʌspekt]	a person considered to have done wrong	Verdächtiger
to put on an act colloq	to behave in an affected way so as to attract attention	sich aufspielen, eine 'Schau abziehen'
bourgeoisie [ˌbuəʒwɑ'ziː]	persons that are mainly concerned with material wealth and social status	Bourgeoisie; (Spieß)bürgertum
to turn upside down	to make or create disorder	alles auf den Kopf stellen
to stand up to s. b.	to resist s. b.	sich gegen jmd stellen; jmd Widerstand leisten
ram a viewpoint up a person's spine	force s. b. to accept some point of view by repeating it continually; cf.: ram s. th. down a person's throat	jmd einen Standpunkt 'einbläuen', 'einbimsen', jmd einen Standpunkt aufdrängen
preservation [ˌprizəː'veiʃən]	act of keeping from loss or decay	Bewahrung, Konservierung, Erhaltung

p. 176

to struggle	to fight	kämpfen
to live one's conviction [kən'vikʃən]	to demonstrate by one's behaviour what one thinks is right	seine Überzeugung vorleben
gear [giə]	a car usually has five gears: first, second, third, fourth, and reverse	Gang (beim Auto)

to shift gears	to adapt one's way of life to circumstances	die Gangart ändern, hier: sich anpassen
to go into reverse [ri'və:s]	to move backwards, to retreat	den Rückwärtsgang einlegen, sich zurückziehen
stock- market	the market where shares are bought and sold, the Stock Exchange for example	Börsenmarkt
ape	a tailless monkey, a primate	Menschenaffe
to confuse s. b.	to mix up a person's mind	jmd verwirren

p. 177

to concede [kən'si:d]	to admit, to agree	zugestehen, zugeben, eingestehen
to propagandize [prɔpə'gændaiz]	to engage in propaganda	propagieren, Propaganda
untoward [ˌʌntə'wɔ:d]	unfavourable, unfortunate, inconvenient	widerspenstig, ungefügig; unglücklich
with an untoward anxiety	his anxiety reveals that he does not agree	etwa: mit ängstlichem Starrsinn
the settlement of the issue is intimate with him	he is personally envolved in the outcome	die Beilegung des Problems berührt ihn persönlich
integrity [in'tegriti]	quality of being honest and upright in character	Rechtschaffenheit. moralische Sauberkeit

p. 178

mourning ['mɔ:niŋ]	grief	Trauer; Kümmernis
to slice s. th.	to cut into slices	etw in Scheiben schneiden
adoration [ˌædə'reiʃən]	worship, love	Anbetung, Verehrung, Bewunderung
to glory in s. th.	to take pride in s. th., to rejoice in s. th.	triumphieren, frohlocken
to grasp [ɑ:]	to seize firmly with the hand or mind	fassen, packen; begreifen
apron ['eiprən]	a garment worn over the front part of the body to keep clothes clean	Schürze

p. 179

to assume a posture of confidence	to adopt an attitude which expresses one's belief in a positive outcome	eine zuversichtliche Haltung annehmen

p. 180

accordion [ə'kɔ:diən]	portable musical instrument with a sort of bellows	Akkordeon
to crane around the corner	to look round the corner by stretching one's neck	seinen Hals recken, um um die Ecke zu schauen
furnace ['fə:nis]	an enclosed fireplace for melting ore	Hoch-, Schmelzofen

a conceivable advantage [kən'si:vəbl]	an advantage that can be understood	ein merklicher Vorteil
a rational explanation ['ræʃənəl ˌeksplə'neiʃən]	an explanation that can be understood with one's intellect	eine vernünftige, rationale Erklärung
atrocity [ə'trɔsiti]	wicked or cruel act; wickedness	Greueltat, Scheußlichkeit
beyond any belief	more than can be believed	unglaublich
vile [vail]	shameful and disgusting	ekelhaft, widerlich
to paralyse ['pærəlaiz]	to make helpless, to prevent from moving	lähmen; stillegen
to despise [dis'paiz]	to look down upon, contempt	verachten

p. 181

the hallmark ['hɔ:lma:k]	mark for indicating the standard of gold and silver	Feingehaltsstempel, Echtheitsstempel
self-restraint ['selfristreint]	keeping oneself under control	Selbstbeherrschung
to guarantee [ˌgærən'ti:]	to give a promise that certain conditions will be fulfilled	garantieren; die Gewähr übernehmen
loss and gain	what is lost and gained in business	Gewinn und Verlust
an inflection [in'flekʃən]	rise and fall of the voice in speaking	Modulation; melodische Intonation

refugee [ˌrefjuːˈdʒiː]	person who has been forced to flee	Flüchtling
to collar s. b.	to seize s. b. by the collar; to get roughly hold of s. b.	'am Kragen packen'

p. 182

bitch	female dog, wolf, or fox; here: spiteful woman or girl	Hündin; Wölfin; Füchsin; hier: Weibsbild, Hure
son-of-a-bitch	American vulgar expression of abuse	Hurensohn; Scheißkerl
to collide with [kəˈlaid]	to come together violently; to be in conflict	zusammenstoßen; kollidieren mit; in Widerspruch stehen
thigh [θai]	upper part of human leg	Oberschenkel
to plead [iː]	here: to ask earnestly and entreatingly	inständig bitten
he jerks him to his feet [dʒəːks]	he gives him a sudden pull so as to make him stand on the feet	er reißt ihn gewaltsam hoch
he leads him out of hearing	he leads him out of hearing distance	er führt ihn außer Hörweite
circumcision [ˌsəːkəmˈsiʒən]	religious rite among Jews and Muslims: the foreskin of a male is removed	Beschneidung
conclusive proof [kənˈkluːsiv]	evidence that ends any possible doubt	schlüssiger, überzeugender Beweis
gentile [ˈdʒentail]	any person not of Jewish race	Nichtjude

p. 183

capricious [kə'priʃəs]	unreliable, often changing one's behaviour without apparent cause	launenhaft, kapriziös
racial anthropology ['reiʃəl ˌænθrəˈpɔlədʒi]	science of man, based on the differences of races	rassische Anthropologie
a line officer	officer on active duty on the front; cf.: combat officer	Frontoffizier
with eyes ablaze	with eyes bright, excited	mit funkelnden Augen
candid ['kændid]	frank, straightforward, honest	offen(herzig), geradeheraus
assignment [ə'sainmənt]	anything given as duty or task	Auftrag, Zuweisung
fragment ['frægmənt]	here: part of a shell	Granatsplitter
to be on loan	to belong somewhere else	ausgeliehen sein
to relieve s. o. from	here: to remove s. o. from his functions	jemanden (seiner Pflichten, Aufgaben, Posten) entheben, entbinden
resentment [ri'zentmənt]	bitter, indignant feeling	Unmut, Groll, Unwille

p. 184

alleyway ['æliwei] Am	narrow passage between two houses	Gasse, Durchgang

pawnshop	a pawnbroker lends money at interest on the security of goods left with him	Pfandleihe
to irritate ['iri,teit]	to make angry	reizen, verärgern, irritieren

p. 185

the Southern Zone ['sʌðən 'zəun]	the territory of France that was not occupied by the German Army during the Second World War	das unbesetzte Frankreich der Vichy-Regierung
to mark out for	to decide in advance that s. o. is going to get some special treatment	für etwas vorherbestimmen
destruction [di'strʌkʃən]	destroying or being destroyed	Zerstörung, Vernichtung, Verwüstung
a general check-up	a general examination of passports	allgemeine Ausweiskontrolle
penis ['pi:nis]	organ of copulation of male animals	Penis, männliches Geschlechtsteil
looking at penises	Jews could be found out that way because of the circumcision	
to overhear [,əuvə'hiə]	to hear without the knowledge of the speaker	belauschen, zufällig mithören
I had Jew stamped on my passport	Jewish passports were specially marked so as to prevent the bearers of these passports to leave the country	

Cyrano de Bergerac [sirɑːˈno də bɛrʒəˈrak]	famous French soldier (1619–1653), some sort of national hero; here: the main character of a play by Edmond Rostant	
Sinclair Lewis [ˈsiŋklɛə ˈluːis]	(1885–1951) American novelist ('Babbit'), Noble Prize winner.	

p. 186

walk-up [ˈ− −]	building of several stories without a lift	Haus ohne fahr- Fahrstuhl, 'Walk-up'
to take turns at/ about going down	first A went down, then B, then A etc.	abwechselnd nach unten gehen
outcry	loud shout or scream; public protest	Aufschrei; Schrei der Entrüstung
remorse [riˈmɔːs]	bitter feeling for having done wrong	Reue, Zerknirschung
urgency [ˈəːdʒənsi]	need for haste or prompt action	Dringlichkeit, Eindringlichkeit, Not
to immobilize [iˈməubilaiz]	to make unable to move	erstarren machen, beweglich machen
to do s. th. purposely [ˈpəːpəsli]	to intend to do s. th., to do it on purpose	etw absichtlich machen
unconscious mind [ʌnˈkɔnʃəs]	here: the mind that works and functions instinctively	der unbewußte Verstand
to wager one's life on [ˈweidʒə]	to bet one's life	um sein Leben wetten
to support	to provide for; to help with money	unterstützen, ernähren

p. 187

oboist ['əubəu,ist]	player of an oboe ['əubəu], a woodwind instrument	Oboespieler, Oboist
beauty mark ['bju:ti,ma:k]	birthmark in the face that bestows some beauty and special charm to women	Schönheits-fleckchen
to slaughter ['slɔ:tə]	to kill animals for food; to butcher	schlachten; hinmorden
assumption [ə'sʌmpʃən]	s. th. taken for granted; supposed, but not proved	Annahme, Vermutung
to bait	to put food on a hook so as to catch fish with it	ködern

p. 188

an able-bodied man	a physically strong man	körperlich kräftiger Mann
aside from me	Am colloq for B. E. besides me	außer mir (einschließend)
I do not fit Am	B. E. I'm not fit for it	ich bin dafür ungeeignet
to assume the worst [ə'sju:m]	to suppose that the worst will happen	das Schlimmste annehmen
desperate ['despərət]	filled with despair and therefore ready to do anything	verzweifelt, rasend, verwegen
freight car Am	goods train	Güterzug
to visualize ['viʒuəlaiz]	to bring as a picture before the mind	sich vergegenwärtigen, sich vorstellen
leading role	the main part in a play	Hauptrolle
fly	flap of cloth on a garment to contain or cover a zip-	Hosenklappe, Hosenlatz

fastener or buttonholes down
the front of a pair of trousers

p. 189

exhaustion [ig′zɔ:stʃən]	total loss of strength	Erschöpfung, Entkräftung
draperies [′dreipəri:z]	material used for garments, hangings, curtains	Textilien, Wollstoffe; Am: Vorhangstoffe
junk [dʒʌŋk]	old discarded things of no value	Plunder, Schund

p. 190

to bait	to put food on a hook so as to catch fish	ködern
to enforce a law	to force people to obey to a law; to impose a law	ein Gesetz durchsetzen
to overthrow a law [,əuvə′θrəu]	to put an end to a law; to abolish a law	ein Gesetz abschaffen
to knock out	to overwhelm, to stun, to knock down	bewußtlos schlagen
to outnumber	to be greater in number than	zahlenmäßig überlegen sein
challenge [′tʃælənd ʒ]	invitation to a personal fight or combat or play	Herausforderung, Aufforderung
subversion [səb′və:ʃən]	act of overthrowing a government by weakening people's confidence and trust	Umsturz, Staatsgefährdung, Subversion
Talmudic [tæl′mu:dik]	derived from Talmud [′tælmud] : the compendium of Jewish law and teaching	talmudisch

to niggle	to give too much time or attention to unimportant details	(pedantisch) herumtüfteln, trödeln

p. 191

he is 'high'	colloq: he is intoxicated sl: he is under the influence of drugs	er ist beschwipst; er ist 'high'
sentry	soldier posted to keep guard	Wachtposten
inconceivable [,inkən'si:vəbl]	that cannot be understood or imagined	unbegreiflich, unfaßbar
manic ['mænik]	showing signs of mania	manisch; irre

p. 192

paw [ɔ:]	animal foot, e. g. a dog's paw	Pfote
with his paws folded	the old Jew's hands are compared to the paws of an animal	
cock vulg sl	penis	vulg. 'Schwanz'
tense in shock	strained to stiffness because of shock	vor Schrecken erstarrt

p. 193

subversive activities [səb'və:siv]	activities aimed at overthrowing the government	umstürzlerische Tätigkeiten
to nudge s. b. [nʌdʒ]	to touch or push slightly with the elbow	mit dem Ellbogen anstoßen

sadism ['seidizm; 'sæ...]	kind of sexual perversion, marked by getting pleasure from cruelty to other persons	Sadismus, perverse Grausamkeit

p. 194

a slight bow [bau]	hardly perceptible inclination of one's head	leichte Verbeugung
to prod s. b. along	to urge s. b. on by pushing him with s. th. pointed	jmd (durch Stöße) vorwärtstreiben

p. 195

with an edgy note of impatience ['edʒi]	showing by one's impatience that one is nervous	mit nervöser Ungeduld
imminent ['iminənt]	going to happen soon	drohend, bevorstehend
summons ['sʌmənz]	order to appear before a judge or somewhere else	Aufforderung, Vorladung, Aufruf
tool shed	place for storing tools	Werkzeugschuppen
resentment [ri'zentmənt]	bitter feeling that one has when insulted or ignored	Groll, verstimmung, Ressentiment
to stick to the rules	to play according to the rules of a game	sich an die Spielregeln halten

p. 196

shred of hope	fragment of hope	Hoffnungsfetzen
to shift about	to keep changing one's position	ständig seine (Ruhe)lage ändern
high tension ['tenʃən]	here: high nervous or emotional strain	nervöse Hochspannung

to be on the verge of [vəːdʒ]	to be close to	am Rande von ... sein
amelioration [ə,miliəˈreiʃən]	becoming better	Verbesserung (der Lage)

p. 197

it's no reflection on you	I don't mean that you are to blame	das soll keine Anspielung auf Sie sein
with an overtone of closeness	with a tone of voice expressing intimacy	in einem vertraulichen Ton
closeness [ˈkləusnis]	intimate friendship, understanding	Vertraulichkeit, persönliche Nähe
agony [ˈægəni]	great pain or suffering of mind or body	Pein, Seelenqual, Todeskampf
hideout [ˈhaidaut]	hiding-place	Versteck
everything is upside down	everything is in complete disorder	alles ist verkehrt; alles 'steht Kopf'
a cynic [ˈsinik]	a person who has no belief in the goodness of man or in human progress	Zyniker

p. 198

to take vengeance on [ˈvendʒəns]	to take revenge on; return injury for injury	Rache nehmen
the scum of mankind [ˈmænkaind]	the worst or seemingly worthless part of the population	Abschaum der Menschheit

to fly out at s. b. Am	to shout angrily at s. b.	jmd anfahren, anschnauzen
to sway	to move from one side to the other	taumeln, wanken

p. 199

with deadened eyes ['dednd]	with expressionless eyes	mit ausdruckslosen Augen
to stain	to make dirty marks on	beflecken, beschmutzen
ineffectual [ˌini'fektjuəl]	having no effect	wirkungslos, kraftlos

p. 200

atrocity [ə'trɔsiti]	wicked, cruel act; wickedness	Scheußlichkeit, Greueltat; Ungeheuerlichkeit
decency ['di:sənsi]	(the quality of) showing what is right and suitable	Anstand, Anständigkeit
implication	here: s. th. hinted at or suggested; hint	Andeutung; eigentliche Bedeutung
monstrousness ['mɔnstrəsnis]	s. th. scandalous causing horror and disgust	Ungeheuerlichkeit, Widernatürlichkeit

p. 201

to see eye to eye with somebody	to agree entirely with s. b., have the same views	mit jmd übereinstimmen; die gleichen Ansichten haben

with your standing	with your social position	bei Ihrer gesellschaftlichen Stellung
abhorrent [əb'hɔrənt]	hateful, causing horror	abscheulich, verhaßt
recognition of authority [ˌrekə'gniʃən]	acknowledgement and acceptance of authority	Autoritätsgläubigkeit, Anerkennung der Autorität

p. 202

clasp knife [ɑ:]	folding-knife	Taschenmesser, Klappmesser
blade	cutting part of a knife	Klinge, Schneide
a plea in his voice	asking a favour by the inflection of his voice	mit bittender Stimme

p. 203

siren ['saiərən]	device for producing a loud shrill noise as a warning	(Alarm)sirene
pursuit [pə'sju:t]	the act of hunting down	Verfolgung
anguish ['æŋgwiʃ]	severe suffering of the mind	(seelische) Angst
incomprehensible [ˌinkɔmpri'hensibl]	that cannot be understood	unbegreiflich, unverständlich

ASCHENDORFFS VOKABULARIEN ZU FREMDSPRACHIGEN TASCHENBÜCHERN

K. Amis: Lucky Jim.
Vokabularien, in Vorbereitung.
Zugrundegelegter Text: Penguin-Taschenbuch ●●

J. Braine: Room at the Top.
Vokabularien, 4./5. Auflage,
160 S., kart. 4,40 DM.
Zugrundegelegter Text: Penguin-Taschenbuch.

T. S. Eliot: The Cocktail Party.
Vokabularien, 72 S., kart. 2,20 DM.
Vokabularien zusammen mit dem ungekürzten Text (Taschenbuch Faber Editions) 6,70 DM.

F. S. Fitzgerald: The Great Gatsby.
Vokabularien, in Vorbereitung.
Zugrundegelegter Text: Penguin-Taschenbuch ●●

William Golding: Lord of the Flies.
Vokabularien, in Vorbereitung.
Zugrundegelegter Text: Faber Editions.

A. Huxley: Brave New World.
Vokabularien, 4./5. Auflage, 78 S., kart. 2,20 DM.
Zugrundegelegter Text: Penguin-Taschenbuch.

New American Drama. E. Albee: The American Dream — J. Richardson: Gallows Humour — M. Schisgal: The Typists — A. Miller: Incident at Vichy.
Vokabularien, 2./3., verbess. Auflage

G. Orwell: Nineteen Eighty-Four.
Vokabularien, 272 S., kart. 8,— DM.
Zugrundegelegter Text: Penguin-Taschenbuch ●●

Verlag Aschendorff
Postfach 11 24, 4400 Münster

J. B. Priestley: Time and the Conways and Other Plays.
Vokabularien, 99 S., kart. 2,80 DM.
Vokabularien zusammen mit dem ungekürzten Text (Penguin-Taschenbuch) 8,90 DM.

G. B. Shaw: Pygmalion.
Vokabularien, 131 S., kart. 3,40 DM.
Zugrundegelegter Text: Penguin-Taschenbuch ●●

J. Wain: Hurry On Down.
Vokabularien, in Vorbereitung.
Zugrundegelegter Text: Penguin-Taschenbuch ●●

E. Waugh: Decline and Fall.
Vokabularien, 95 S., kart. 2,80 DM.
Vokabularien zusammen mit dem ungekürzten Text (Penguin-Taschenbuch) 6,60 DM.

E. Waugh: The Loved One.
Vokabularien, 131 S., kart. 4,— DM.
Zugrundegelegter Text: Penguin-Taschenbuch ●●

A. Camus: La Peste.
Vokabularien, 208 S., kart. 5,80 DM.
Zugrundegelegter Text: Folio-Taschenbuch ●

J. Cocteau: Les Parents terribles.
Vokabularien, 63 S., kart. 2,— DM.
Zugrundegelegter Text: Folio-Taschenbuch ●

J. P. Sartre: Les Jeux sont faits.
Vokabularien, 76 S., kart. 2,20 DM.
Zugrundegelegter Text: Taschenbuch aus dem Verlag Nagel, Paris.

● französisches Taschenbuch = Bezug durch: Saarbach, Postfach 10 16 10, 5000 Köln 1

●● englisches Taschenbuch = Bezug durch Buchimport Hans Heinrich Petersen, Postfach 53 02 30, 2000 Hamburg 53